Fundamentals of
PROJECT
MANAGEMENT

SIXTH EDITION

Fundamentals of
PROJECT
MANAGEMENT

SIXTH EDITION

JOSEPH HEAGNEY

HarperCollins
LEADERSHIP

AN IMPRINT OF HarperCollins

Published by HarperCollins Leadership, an imprint of HarperCollins Focus LLC.

Any internet addresses, phone numbers, or company or product information printed in this book are offered as a resource and are not intended in any way to be or to imply an endorsement by HarperCollins Leadership, nor does HarperCollins Leadership vouch for the existence, content, or services of these sites, phone numbers, companies, or products beyond the life of this book.

This publication is designed to provide accurate and authoritative information in regard to the subject matter covered. It is sold with the understanding that the publisher is not engaged in rendering legal, accounting, or other professional service. If legal advice or other expert assistance is required, the services of a competent professional person should be sought.

"PMI" and the PMI logo are service and trademarks of the Project Management Institute, Inc., which are registered in the United States of America and other nations; "PMP" and the PMP logo are certification marks of the Project Management Institute, Inc., which are registered in the United States of America and other nations; "PMBOK," "PM Network," and "PMI Today" are trademarks of the Project Management Institute, Inc., which are registered in the United States of America and other nations; ". . . building professionalism in project management . . ." is a trade and service mark of the Project Management Institute, Inc., which is registered in the United States of America and other nations; and the Project Management Journal logo is a trademark of the Project Management Institute, Inc.

PMI did not participate in the development of this publication and has not reviewed the content for accuracy. PMI does not endorse or otherwise sponsor this publication and makes no warranty, guarantee, or representation, expressed or implied, as to its accuracy or content. PMI does not have any financial interest in this publication, and has not contributed any financial resources.

Additionally, PMI makes no warranty, guarantee, or representation, expressed or implied, that the successful completion of any activity or program, or the use of any product or publication, designed to prepare candidates for the PMP® Certification Examination, will result in the completion or satisfaction of any PMP® Certification eligibility requirement or standard.

ISBN 978-1-4002-3532-2 (eBook)
ISBN 978-1-4002-3526-1 (TP)

Library of Congress Control Number: 2016004879

Printed in the United States of America
24 25 26 27 28 LBC 6 5 4 3 2

To Mom and Dad—the best

CONTENTS

FIGURE LIST

PREFACE TO THE SIXTH EDITION

The year 2021 is past; it is 2022—fantastic! It is time to focus on recovery, renewal, and superior project performance, on time, on budget, and with excellent deliverables. Unfortunately, organizations throughout the world will be absorbing the lagging impact of the pandemic, its economic fallout, and the normal rate of change that never changes, but seems only to accelerate. For project managers, recent events have added to our challenges. Pandemic-related recovery plans, project resource upheaval, as well as increased reliance on virtual teams will be on the agenda for most project managers in the coming years. The new edition of *Fundamentals of Project Management* will provide valuable information for project managers to navigate this challenging project world. There will be expanded focus on the "Pulse of the Profession Report 2021" as presented by the Project Management Institute. Although many planned projects were put on hold, an increased number were completed on time and within budget while meeting their goals, compared with last year's "Pulse" data. The report reflects other key trends in the world of project management and serves as an important guide for beginners and veterans alike. This sixth edition will address all of the above, and update data and processes presented in the fifth edition to guide you through this new decade.

The section "Working with Virtual Teams" in chapter 14 has been enhanced by offering additional tools and tactics for effectively leading collocated project teams and communicating in a virtual environment. The trend continues for projects to include team members distributed throughout the state, country, or world. The pandemic of 2020–22, continued globalization, and the explosion of teleworking are presenting unique challenges for project leaders everywhere. Much has changed with project human resources stretched and in a constant state of flux, budgets slashed, and, in many cases, major shifts in high-level strategic plans affecting projects throughout the organization. Improved technology brings increased capability and challenges and requires adjustments to maximize the capability of the new tools. Shiny new project software does not manage projects, people do. This expanded section will offer best practices for the project manager to address these issues as well as traps to avoid in the new environment.

To address the project world of the 2020s, "Project Recovery" has been added to this edition as a new chapter. Effective recovery begins with an accurate assessment of the current state of the project. This enables project managers to understand priorities and maximize resources as the recovery road map is created. The FADE process provides structure for this map and is introduced here. This will be presented in the context of project management process *and* leadership. A confluence of the two is necessary for project managers to correct course and move forward. Successful recovery includes re-planning and managing the reset as one would any project; plan/schedule/control the recovery. Too many projects have been sucked into the vortex of a *faulty fix* with no idea regarding what happened or what to do about it. This chapter will provide crucial information for all project managers struggling with these challenges and will include a focus on managing risk during recovery. Always important, project risk management becomes indispensable in any project recovery effort to ensure that the cure is not worse than what ails the project. Project termination, that most difficult of project decisions, will conclude this timely and important chapter.

Why project management and why this book? Because the tools and techniques that one hones through project experience can be applied in *any* industry on *any* level, anywhere in the world.

Start with the *Fundamentals of Project Management*, manage your projects accordingly, and you will be better equipped for success throughout your career.

JOSEPH J. HEAGNEY
August 2022

CHAPTER 1

AN OVERVIEW OF PROJECT MANAGEMENT

What's all the fuss about, anyway? Since the first edition of this book was published, in 1997, the Project Management Institute (PMI) has grown from a few thousand members to over six hundred thousand worldwide and more than three hundred local chapters in 2021. For those of you who don't know, PMI is the professional organization for people who manage projects. You can get more information from the institute's website, www.pmi.org. In addition to providing a variety of member services, a major objective of PMI is to advance project management as a profession. To do so, it has established a certification process whereby qualifying individuals receive the Project Management Professional (PMP®) designation. To do so, such individuals must have work experience (between thirty-six and sixty months leading projects, depending upon education), thirty-five hours of project management education/training (or CAPM certification), and pass an exam that is based on the *Project Management Body of Knowledge (PMBOK®) Guide.* The most recent version of the *PMBOK* (seventh edition) includes a significant shift from Knowledge Areas to Project Performance Domains.

A professional association? Just for project management? Isn't project management just a variant on general management?

Yes and no. There are a lot of similarities, but there are enough differences to justify treating project management as a discipline separate from general management. For one thing, projects are more schedule-intensive than most of the activities that general managers handle. And the people in a project team often don't report directly to the project manager, whereas they do report to most general managers.

So, just what is project management, and, for that matter, what is a project? PMI defines a project as "a temporary endeavor undertaken to create a unique product, service, or result" (*PMBOK® Guide*, PMI, 2021, p. 245). This means that a project is done only one time. If it is repetitive, it's not a project. A project should have definite starting and ending points (time), a budget (cost), a clearly defined scope—or magnitude—of work to be done, and specific performance requirements that must be met. I say "should" because seldom does a project conform to the desired definition. These constraints on a project, by the way, are referred to throughout this book as the PCTS (performance, cost, time, scope) targets.

> PMI defines a project as "a temporary endeavor undertaken to produce a unique product, service, or result."

Dr. J. M. Juran, the late quality management guru, also defines a project as a problem scheduled for solution. I like this definition because it reminds me that every project is conducted to solve some kind of problem for a company. However, I must caution that the word "problem" typically has a negative meaning, and projects deal with both positive and negative kinds of problems.

For example, developing a new product is a problem, but a positive one, while an environmental cleanup project deals with a negative kind of problem.

"A project is a problem scheduled for solution."

—J. M. JURAN

Project Failures and Success

Current studies indicate mixed results regarding project management success rates. According to TeamStage, a provider of project management software, an eye-opening 70 percent of all projects fail to deliver what was promised to project customers. TeamStage also reports that 42 percent of organizations do not understand the importance of project management and 55 percent of project managers cite budget overruns as the reason for project failure. IT projects can be especially challenging today. Steve Andriole, enterprise tech contributor to Forbes.com, notes, "A survey published in HBR found that the average IT project overran its budget by 27 percent. Moreover, at least one in six IT projects turns into a 'black swan' with a cost overrun of 200 percent and a schedule overrun of 70 percent."

Most telling were the data recently reported by the Project Management Institute. PMI consistently measures the state of project, program, and portfolio management. Their 2021 "Pulse of the Profession" study (Beyond Agility: Flex to the Future 2021) reveals some positive trends, with projects overall experiencing on-time completion rates of 55 percent and within budget rates of 62 percent. Approximately 73 percent of projects met their original goals and business intent.

This report has also identified the emergence of what PMI calls gymnastic enterprises. Gymnastic enterprises are "those that have learned to flex and pivot wherever and whenever needed—while maintaining structure, form, and governance." Compared to traditional enterprises, these will focus on organizational agility. Gymnastic enterprises are also more likely to use standardized risk management practices (see chapter 6). Both organizational agility and robust risk management practices were significant drivers of project success across the "Pulse of the Profession" respondent base. Today's project manager should take note of the advantages of approaching their projects with agility in mind, ready to flex and pivot as necessary.

My own survey, based on thirty-five years of project management, best practice identification, project consulting, and training, reveals that the more things change, the more they stay the same. Not enough planning is being accomplished. Large or small, software, R&D, or administrative, successful projects rely on good *planning*. Too many project managers take a ready-fire-aim approach in an attempt to complete a project quickly. Many organizations do not allow project managers significant planning time or virtually any time at all. This often results in spending far more time and effort reworking errors, soothing unhappy stakeholders, and backing out of blind alleys. In short, the lack of adequate planning causes projects to fail.

What Is Project Management?

The *PMBOK® Guide* definition of project management is the "application of knowledge, skills, tools, and techniques to project activities to meet the project requirements" (*PMBOK® Guide*, PMI, 2021, p. 245). Examples of typical projects include an annual senior management conference, adding multiple languages to user manuals, the development of software, and improving manufacturing cycle–time, to name a few.

> "Project management is the application of knowledge, skills, tools, and techniques to project activities to meet the project requirements."
> —*PMBOK® GUIDE*

While the previous edition of *PMBOK* was project manager and process focused, the most recent *PMBOK* is project team and outcome focused. The five process groups of the sixth edition have been replaced by twelve Project Delivery Principles. These principles "are built around a set of statements that guide the actions and behaviors of project management practitioners regardless of development approach." The twelve principles are:

- Stewardship
- Team
- Stakeholders
- Value
- Holistic Thinking
- Quality
- Complexity
- Leadership
- Tailoring
- Opportunities and Threats
- Adaptability and Resilience
- Change Management

The seventh edition of *PMBOK* has also replaced the ten Knowledge Areas with eight Performance Domains. PMI defines a Performance Domain as "groups of related activities that are critical for the effective delivery of project outcomes." The eight domains are:

- Team
- Stakeholders

- Life Cycle
- Planning
- Navigating Uncertainty and Ambiguity
- Delivery
- Performance
- Project Work

These changes reflect the global shift in project management itself. As stated in the "Pulse of the Profession" report, agility and flexibility are required to be successful in today's organizational and project environment.

It would be better if the *PMBOK® Guide* specified that a project manager should facilitate planning. One mistake made by inexperienced project managers is to plan the projects for their teams. Not only do they get no buy-in to their plans, but their plans are usually full of holes. Managers can't think of everything, their estimates of task durations are wrong, and everything falls apart after the projects are started. The first rule of project management is that the people who must do the work should help plan it.

> **The first rule of project management is that the people who must do the work should help plan it.**

The role of the project manager is that of an enabler. Her job is to help the team get the work completed, to "run interference" for the team, to get scarce resources that team members need, and to buffer them from outside forces that would disrupt the work. She is not a project czar. She should be—above all else—a *leader*, in the truest sense of the word.

The best definition of leadership that I have found is the one by Vance Packard, in his book *The Pyramid Climbers* (Crest Books, 1962). He says, "Leadership is the art of getting others to want to do something that you believe should be done." The operative word here is "want." Dictators get others to do things that they want done. So do guards who supervise prison work teams. But a leader gets people to want to do the work, and that is a significant difference.

> "Leadership is the art of getting others to want to do something that you believe should be done."
>
> —VANCE PACKARD

The planning, scheduling, and control of work represent the management or administrative parts of the job. But, without leadership, projects tend to just satisfy bare minimum requirements. With leadership, they can exceed those bare minimums. I offer a comprehensive application of project leadership techniques in chapter 14.

It Is Not Just Scheduling!

One of the common misconceptions about project management is that it is just scheduling. At last report, Microsoft had sold a huge number of copies of Microsoft Project®, yet the project failure rate remains high. Scheduling is certainly a major tool used to manage projects, but it is not nearly as important as developing a shared understanding of what the project is supposed to accomplish or constructing a good work breakdown structure (WBS) to identify all the work to be done (I discuss the WBS in chapter 7). In fact, without practicing good project management, the only thing a detailed schedule is going to do is allow you to document your failures with great precision!

I do want to make one point about scheduling software. It doesn't matter too much which package you select, as they all have strong and weak points. However, the tendency is to give people the software and expect them to learn how to use it without any training. This simply does not work. The features of scheduling software are such that most people don't learn the subtleties by themselves. They don't have the time because they are trying to do their regular jobs, and not everyone is good at self-paced learning. You wouldn't hire a green person to run a complex machine in a factory and put him to work without training because you know he will destroy something or injure himself. So why do it with software?

The Accidental Project Manager

Have you been suddenly thrust into the role of managing a project without the title "project manager" or much support? Did you consider yourself the project manager *and* the project team? You are not alone. Increasingly, individuals are managing work that fits the *PMBOK® Guide* (PMI 7, 2021) definition of a project: "a temporary endeavor undertaken to create a unique product, service, or result." There is a deadline, a scope of work to define, limited resources, and often a fixed budget. Although less formal and not requiring a project team, these projects must be planned, scheduled, and controlled. An exceptional/acceptable project product must be delivered and the customer delighted or at least satisfied.

"Essentials of Project Management for the Nonproject Manager" is a seminar that I lead for American Management Association International. It is very popular and has struck a chord with nontraditional project managers, subject matter experts, sponsors, and project contributors. Typical attendees include sales managers, administrative professionals, marketing managers, procurement specialists, and many other business types. It seems that everyone is involved with projects on some level. These attendees are not project managers in the traditional sense but must manage projects. Project management tools can help. I like to tell my attendees that project tools are universal but the value is evident in how the tools are applied.

First, assess the work. Are you constrained by scope, cost, and limited resources? Do you have a deadline? Then commit to managing the work as a project. Determine which project tools would be appropriate. For example, a project with a deadline of two weeks requires far fewer project management applications than a project due in fifty weeks. Streamline or expand your management approach to align with the length, width, depth, and breadth of the project.

The Big Trap: Working Project Managers

It is common to have individuals serve as project managers and also require that they do part of the actual work in the project. This is a certain prescription for problems. If it is a true team, consisting of several people, the project manager inevitably finds herself torn between managing and getting her part of the work done. Naturally, the work must take precedence or the schedule will slip, so she opts to do the work. That means that the managing does not get done. She hopes it will take care of itself, but it never does. After all, if the team could manage itself, there would be no need for a project manager in the first place. (Remember our argument about whether project management matters?)

Unfortunately, when the time comes for her performance evaluation, she will be told that her managing needs improving. Actually, she just needs to be allowed to practice management in the first place.

Yes, for very small teams—perhaps up to three or four people—a project manager can do some of the work. But, as team sizes increase, it becomes impossible to both work and manage because you are constantly being pulled away from the work by the needs of your team members.

One of the reasons for this situation is that organizations don't fully understand what project management is all about, and they think that it is possible for individuals to do both. The result is that nearly everyone in the company is trying to manage projects, and, as is true in every discipline, some of them will be good at it and others will have no aptitude whatsoever. I have found that a far better approach is to select a few individuals who have the aptitude and desire to be project managers and let them manage a number of small projects. This frees "technical" people (to use the term broadly) to do technical work without having to worry about administrative issues, while allowing project managers to get really good at their jobs.

It is outside the scope of this book to discuss how to select project managers, but, for the interested reader, the topic is covered in a book by J. Rodney Turner, PhD, and Ralf Muller, DBA, titled *Choosing Appropriate Project Managers* (Project Management Institute, 2006).

You Can't Have It All!

One of the common causes of project failures is that the project sponsor demands that the project manager must finish the job by a certain time, within budget, and at a given magnitude or scope, while achieving specific performance levels. In other words, the sponsor dictates all four of the project constraints. This doesn't work.

The relationship among the P, C, T, and S constraints can be written as follows:

$$C = f(x)(P, T, S)$$

In words, cost is a function of performance, time, and scope. Graphically, I like to show it as a triangle, in which P, C, and T are the sides and S is the area. This is shown in figure 1-1.

In geometry, we know that if we are given values for the sides of a triangle, we can compute the area. Or, if we know the area and the length of two sides, we can compute the length of the remaining side. This translates into a very practical rule of project management: the sponsor can assign values to any three variables, but the project manager must determine the remaining one.

So let's assume that the sponsor requires certain performance, time, and scope parameters for the project. It is the project manager's job to determine what it will cost to achieve those results.

[FIGURE 1-1]

TRIANGLES SHOWING THE RELATIONSHIPS AMONG P, C, T, AND S

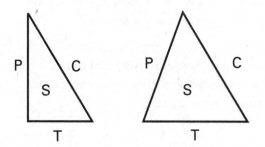

However, I always caution project managers that they should have a paramedic standing by when they give the cost figure to the sponsor because she will probably have a stroke or heart attack, and the paramedic will have to revive her.

Invariably, the sponsor exclaims, "How can it cost that much?" She had a figure in mind, and your number will always exceed her figure. And she may say, "If it's going to cost that much, we can't justify doing the job." Exactly! And that is the decision she should make. But she is certain to try to get the project manager to commit to a lower number, and, if you do, then you only set up yourself—and her—to take a big fall later on.

It is your *obligation* to give the sponsor a valid cost so that she can make a valid decision about whether the project should be done. If you allow yourself to be intimidated into committing to a lower number, it is just going to be a disaster later on, and you are far better off taking your lumps now than being hanged later on.

Of course, there is another possibility. If she says she can afford only so much for the job, then you can offer to reduce the scope. If the job is viable at that scope level, then the project can be done. Otherwise, it is prudent to forget this project and do something else that can make a profit for the company. As someone has said, there is a higher probability that things will accidentally go wrong in a project than that they will accidently go right. In terms of cost estimates, this means that there is always a higher likelihood that the budget will be overrun than that the project will come in under budget. This is just another way of stating Murphy's law: "Whatever can go wrong will go wrong."

> **There is a higher probability that things will accidentally go wrong in a project than that they will accidentally go right.**

The Phases of a Project

There are many different models for the phases a project goes through during its life cycle. One of these that captures the all-too-frequent nature of projects that are not managed well is shown in figure 1-2.

[FIGURE 1-2]
LIFE CYCLE OF A TROUBLED PROJECT

I have shown this diagram to people all over the world, and they invariably laugh and say, "Yes, that's the way it works." I suppose the comfort I can take is that we Americans are not the only ones who have the problem, but the bad news is that there are a lot of dysfunctional projects if everyone recognizes the model.

At the simplest level, a project has a beginning, middle, and end. I prefer the life-cycle model shown in figure 1-3, but other versions are equally valid. In my model, you will notice that every project begins as a concept, which is always "fuzzy," and that the project team must formalize the definition of the job before doing any work. However, because of our ready-fire-aim mentality, we often start working on the job without ensuring that we have a proper definition or that everyone shares the mission and vision for the job. This invariably leads to major problems as the project progresses. This is illustrated by the example that follows.

[FIGURE 1-3]

APPROPRIATE PROJECT LIFE CYCLE

CONCEPT	DEFINITION	PLANNING	EXECUTION	CLOSEOUT
Marketing Input Survey of Competition	Define Problem Develop Vision Write Mission Statement	Develop Strategy Implementation Planning Risk Management	Do All Work Monitor Progress Corrective Action	Final Reports Lessons-Learned Review

EFFORT EXPENDED IN PLANNING

Definition

Some years ago, a project manager in one of my client companies called me and said, "I've just had a conference call with key members of my project team, and I realized that we don't agree on what the project is supposed to accomplish."

I assured him that this was common.

"What should I do?" he asked.

I told him that he had no choice but to get the team members all going in the same direction by clarifying the mission of the project. He asked me to facilitate a meeting to do this.

At the meeting, I stood in front of a flip chart and began by saying, "Let's write a problem statement." Someone immediately countered by saying, "We don't need to do that. We all know what the problem is."

I was unmoved by this comment. I said, "Well, if that is true, it's just a formality and will only take a few minutes, and it would help me if we wrote it down. So someone help me get started."

I'm going to be a little facetious to illustrate what happened next. Someone said, "The," and I wrote the word on the chart, and someone else said, "I don't agree with that!"

Three hours later, we finally finished writing a problem statement.

The project manager was right. The team did not agree on what the problem was, much less how to solve it. This is fundamental—and is so often true that I have begun to think we have a defective gene in all of us that prohibits us from insisting that we have a good definition of the problem before we start the work. Remember, project management is solving a problem on a large scale, and the way you define a problem determines how you will solve it. If you have the wrong definition, you may come up with the right solution—to the wrong problem!

In fact, I have become convinced that projects seldom fail at the end. Rather, they fail during the definition phase. As the name implies, the *definition* phase of a project occurs very early when the problem is defined, the vision is developed, and the mission becomes clear. I call projects without clear definitions headless-chicken projects because they are like the chicken that has had its head chopped off and runs around spewing blood everywhere before it finally falls over and is "officially" dead. Projects work the same way. They spew blood all over the place until someone finally says, "I think that project is dead," and indeed it is. But it was actually dead when we chopped off its head in the beginning—it just took a while for everyone to realize it (see chapter 17).

Once the project is defined, you can plan how to do the work. There are three components to the plan: strategy, tactics, and logistics. Strategy is the overall approach or "game plan" that will be followed to do the work. The following example of strategy was related to me by a friend who is into military history.

Strategy

The *strategy* phase of a project determines the high-level approach that your project will take to achieve the project requirements. A good example is the case of Avondale Shipyard. During World War II, defense contractors were under great pressure to build weaponry at intense levels. To accelerate the construction of ships and planes in particular, many new assembly methods were invented. Avondale Shipyard, on the Mississippi River north of New Orleans, for example, worked on a new method of building ships. The traditional way had always been to build the ship in an upright position. However, ships built of steel require welding in the bottom, or keel area, of the boat, and this was very difficult to do. Avondale decided to build its ships upside down, to make the welding easier, and then turn them over to complete the structures above the top deck. This strategy was so effective that Avondale could build boats faster, cheaper, and of higher quality than their competitors, and the strategy is still being used today, more than seventy years later.

Implementation Planning

The *implementation planning* phase of a project includes tactics and logistics. If you are going to build boats upside down, you must work out the details of how it will be done. A fixture must be constructed that will hold the boat and allow it to be turned over without being damaged. This is called working out the tactics. It also includes the sequence in which the work will be done, who will do what, and how long each step will take.

Logistics deals with making sure the team has the materials and other supplies needed to do their jobs. Ordinarily, we think about providing teams with the raw materials they need, but if the project is in a location where they can't get food, work will soon come to a grinding halt. So, provisions must be made for the team to be fed—and possibly housed.

Execution and Control

Once the plan has been developed and approved, the team can begin work. This is the *execution* phase of the project, but it also includes *control* because, while the plan is being implemented, progress is monitored to ensure that the work is progressing according to the plan. When deviations from the plan occur, corrective action is taken to get the project back on track, or, if this is not possible, the plan is changed and approved, and the revised plan becomes the new baseline against which progress is tracked.

Closeout

When all the work has been completed, the *closeout* phase requires that a review of the project be conducted. The purpose is to learn lessons from this job that can be applied to future ones. Two questions are asked: "What did we do well?" and "What do we want to improve next time?"

Notice that we don't ask what was done wrong. This question tends to make people defensive, and they try to hide things that may result in their being punished. In fact, a lessons-learned review should never be conducted in a blame-and-punishment mode. If you are trying to conduct an inquisition, that's different. The purpose of an inquisition is usually to find who is responsible for major disasters and punish them. Lessons-learned sessions should be exactly what the words imply.

I have learned during the past few years that very few organizations do regular lessons-learned reviews of their projects. There is a reluctance to "open a can of worms." And there is a desire to get on with the next job. The problem is that you are almost sure to repeat the mistakes made on the previous project if no one knows about them or has an understanding of how they happened so that they can determine how to prevent them. But, perhaps most important, you can't even take advantage of the good things you did if you don't know about them.

It has been said that the organizations that survive and thrive in the future will be those that learn faster than their competitors. This seems especially true for projects.

The Steps in Managing a Project

The actual steps in managing a project are straightforward. Accomplishing them may not be. The model in figure 1-4 illustrates the steps.

Subsequent chapters of this book elaborate on how each step is accomplished. For now, here is a brief description of the actions involved.

[FIGURE 1-4]

THE STEPS IN MANAGING A PROJECT

Define the Problem

As discussed previously, you need to identify the problem to be solved by the project. It helps to visualize the desired end result. What will be different? What will you see, hear, taste, touch, or smell? (Use sensory evidence if things can't be quantified.) What client need is being satisfied by the project?

Develop Solution Options

How many different ways might you go about solving the problem? Brainstorm solution alternatives (you can do this alone or as a group). Of the available alternatives, which do you think will best solve the problem? Is it more or less costly than other suitable choices? Will it result in a complete or only a partial fix?

Plan the Project

Planning is answering questions: What must be done, by whom, for how much, how, when, and so on? Naturally, answering these questions often requires a crystal ball. We discuss these steps in more detail in chapters 2, 3, and 5.

Execute the Plan

Obviously. Once the plan is drafted, it must be implemented. Interestingly, we sometimes find people going to great effort to put together a plan, then failing to follow it. If a plan is not followed, there is not much point in planning, is there?

Monitor and Control Progress

Plans are developed so that you can achieve your end result successfully. Unless progress is monitored, you cannot be sure you will succeed. It would be like having a road map to a destination but not monitoring the highway signs along the way.

Of course, if a deviation from the plan is discovered, you must ask what must be done to get back on track or—if that seems impossible—how the plan should be modified to reflect new realities.

Close the Project

Once the destination has been reached, the project is finished, but a final step should be taken. Some people call it an audit, others a postmortem (sounds a bit morbid, doesn't it?). Whatever you call it, the point is to learn something from what you just did. Note the way the questions are phrased: "What was done well? What should be improved? What else did we learn?" We can always improve on what we have done. However, asking, "What did we do wrong?" is likely to make people a bit defensive, so the focus should be on improvement, not on placing blame. More on this later.

The Project Management Body of Knowledge (PMBOK®) Guide

The Project Management Institute has attempted to determine a minimum body of knowledge that a project manager needs in order to be effective. As mentioned earlier when I defined project management, the new *PMBOK® Guide* (seventh edition) has identified eight Project Performance Domains. Remember, these domains are defined as "a group of related activities that are critical for the effective delivery of project outcomes." Each addresses activities and functions associated with that specific domain. I will provide a portion of the PMI summary for each. If you want a complete document, you can get one by visiting PMI's website.

Stakeholder

This domain is, appropriately, all about stakeholders. Effective stakeholder interaction is a major contributing factor to successful project outcomes. Stakeholder engagement includes implementing strategies and actions to promote productive involvement of stakeholders in project decision making and implementation.

Team

The Team Performance Domain focuses on the people who are responsible for producing project deliverables that realize business outcomes. This includes fostering team development, encouraging leadership behaviors from all project team members, and sharing ownership for the outcomes.

Development Approach and Life Cycle

This domain addresses the development approach, cadence, and life cycle phases of the project. Deliverables determine the most appropriate development approach such as predictive, adaptive, or hybrid. The development approach and delivery cadence influence the project life cycle and its phases.

Planning

The Planning Domain involves the initial, ongoing, and evolving organization and coordination necessary for delivering project deliverables and outcomes. Planning organizes, elaborates, and coordinates work throughout the project life cycle. Planning takes place up front and throughout the project.

Project Work

This domain includes establishing project processes, managing physical resources, and fostering a learning environment. The focus here is process establishment and performing the work to enable the team to deliver the expected value and project outcomes.

Delivery

The Delivery Performance Domain focuses on delivery of the scope and quality that the project was undertaken to achieve. Projects support strategy execution and advancing business objectives. This domain addresses meeting requirements, scope, and quality expectations to deliver the outputs that will drive intended outcomes.

Measurement

This domain provides a focus on project performance and taking appropriate actions to maintain acceptable performance. Measurement involves assessing project performance and implementing appropriate responses to maintain optimal performance.

Uncertainty

The Uncertainty Performance Domain involves a focus on risk and uncertainty. Projects exist in environments with varying degrees of risk and uncertainty. This presents threats and opportunities that project teams research and assess and then decide how to handle.

KEY POINTS TO REMEMBER

- A project is a temporary endeavor undertaken to produce a unique product, service, or result.
- A project is also a problem scheduled for solution.
- Project management is the application of knowledge, skills, tools, and techniques to project activities to meet the project requirements.
- All projects are constrained by performance, time, cost, and scope requirements. Only three of these can have values assigned. The fourth must be determined by the project team.
- Projects tend to fail because the team does not take the time to ensure that they have developed a proper definition of the problem being solved.
- The major phases of a project include concept, definition, planning, execution, control, and closeout.
- Project stakeholders must be identified *and* managed.

EXERCISES

1. Project management is not just:
   a. Planning.
   b. Rework.
   c. Scheduling.
   d. Controlling.
2. The problem with being a working project manager is that, in a conflict between working and managing:
   a. You don't know what priorities to set.
   b. Your boss will think you're slacking off.
   c. There will never be enough time to do both.
   d. The work will take precedence, and managing will suffer.

3. The *PMBOK® Guide* refers to:

   a. The body of knowledge identified by PMI as needed by project managers to be effective.

   b. A test administered by PMI to certify project managers.

   c. An acronym for a special kind of risk analysis, like FMEA (Failure Mode and Effects Analysis).

   d. None of the above.

4. Project scope defines:

   a. A project manager's line of sight to the end date.

   b. The magnitude or size of the job.

   c. How often a project has been changed.

   d. The limits of a project manager's authority.

CHAPTER 2

THE ROLE OF THE PROJECT MANAGER

The role of project managers seems to be very misunderstood throughout the world. Because many project managers arrive at their positions as a natural progression from their jobs as engineers, programmers, scientists, and other kinds of jobs, both they and their bosses see the job as technical. This simply isn't true.

The primary responsibility of the project manager is to ensure that all work is completed on time, within budget and scope, and at the correct performance level.

If you remember that every project produces a product, service, or result, then there is a technical aspect to the job. However, it is a question of who is responsible for what, and project managers who must manage the project and handle technical issues are set up to fail from the beginning. I will fully explain this later on. For now, suffice it to say that the primary responsibility of the project manager is to ensure that all work is completed on time, within budget and scope, and at the correct performance level. That is, she must see that the PCTS targets are met. Her primary role is to manage the project, not do the work!

What Is Managing?

The PMI definition of project management does not completely capture the true nature of project management. Remember, it says that "project management is the application of knowledge, skills, tools, and techniques to project activities to meet the project requirements" (*PMBOK® Guide*, PMI, 2021, p. 245). PMI has also added Project Delivery Principles and eight Performance Domains to guide the project manager. That sounds nice on paper, but what is it that a person really does when he manages?

I don't know if it is really possible to convey what managing actually is. One reason is that project management is a performing art, and it is difficult to convey in words what an actor, athlete, or artist does. However, we can describe the various roles of a project manager, and that is the focus of this chapter. What should be clear is that you can't very well become something if you can't describe and define it, so this is a necessary exercise.

Definitions of Management

One common definition of management says that a manager gets work done by other people. Only a bit of thought is needed to realize how useless this definition is. Dictators get work done by other people, but I wouldn't call that management. Dr. Peter Drucker, whom many credit with being the "father" of management because he first made people realize that management was a profession rather than a job, has said that a manager is supposed to make an unsolicited contribution to the organization. That is, a manager looks around to see what needs to be done to advance the cause of the organization and does it without asking permission or having to be told to do it. This is often called being proactive, as opposed to reactive, and it is.

But, most important, a manager can't do this unless she understands the mission and vision for the organization and takes initiative to help achieve them. And I believe this applies equally well to project managers. First, they must understand the mission and vision of the organization; then they must see how the project they are managing meshes with the organization's mission; then they must steer the project to ensure that the interests of the organization are met.

> **First, project managers must understand the mission and vision of the organization; then they must see how the project they are managing meshes with the organization's mission; then they must steer the project to ensure that the interests of the organization are met.**

It's About People!

In addition, I said earlier that project management is not a technical job. It is about getting people to perform work that must be done to meet the objectives of the project. In that respect, the classical definition is correct, but Drucker has pointed out that the manager must get people to perform above the minimum acceptable performance level. The reason is that this minimum level is the survival level for the organization, and any company that just manages to survive will not do so for long. Eventually the competition will pass it by, and the organization will die.

So the first skills that a project manager needs are people skills. Herein lies the source of major problems for many project managers—and general managers, too, for that matter. I have found that most managers know more about getting performance from computers, machines, and money than they do about getting people to perform. There are many reasons for this, but chief among them is that nobody has ever taught them practical methods for dealing with people, and we simply aren't born knowing how. So far as I know, the geneticists have not yet found a people-skills gene that endows a person with these skills.

Furthermore, many project managers who have strong technical backgrounds find it difficult to deal with people effectively. They are things oriented, not people oriented, and some will even go so far as to say that they hate this aspect of the job. My recommendation is that they forget about being project managers if this is true. You usually aren't very effective at something you hate doing, but, beyond that, why spend your life doing something you hate?

The Working Project Manager

In fact, one of the biggest traps for project managers is to be what is euphemistically called a *working project manager*. This means that the project manager is indeed responsible for performing technical work in addition to managing the job. The problem with this is that when there is a conflict between managing and doing work—and there always is such a conflict—the work will take priority, and the managing will be neglected. However, when it comes time for the manager's performance appraisal, he will be told that his technical work was okay, but the managing was inadequate. This is a double bind that should not exist.

Authority

The universal complaint from project managers is that they have a lot of responsibility but no authority. This is true, and it is not likely to change. It is the nature of the job, I'm afraid. However, you can't delegate responsibility without giving a person the authority commensurate with the responsibility you want him to take, so, while the project manager's authority might be limited, it cannot be zero.

A word to project managers, however. I learned early in my career as an engineer that you have as much authority as you are willing to take. I know that sounds strange. We see authority as something granted to us by the organization, but it turns out that those individuals who take authority for granted usually get it officially. Of course, I am not advocating that you violate any of the policies of the organization. That is not a proper use of authority. But when it comes to making decisions, rather than checking with your boss to see if something is okay, make the decision yourself, take action that is appropriate and does not violate policy, and then inform your boss what you have done. Many managers have told me that they wish their people would quit placing all decisions on their shoulders to make. And they wish their people would bring them solutions rather than problems. In other words, your boss is looking for you to take some of the load and leave her free to do other things.

A Moment of Truth

Jan Carlzon was the youngest ever CEO of Scandinavian Airlines, and he successfully turned around the ailing airline. He did so in part by empowering all employees to do their jobs without having to ask permission for every action they felt they should take to meet customer needs. He pointed out that every interaction between an employee and a customer was a moment of truth in which the customer would evaluate the airline's service. If that service was good, then the customer would be likely to fly SAS again; conversely, if it wasn't good, the customer would be less likely to do so. As Carlzon pointed out, from the customer's point of view, the SAS employee *is* the airline.

Furthermore, Carlzon revised the standard organization chart, which is typically a triangle with the CEO at the apex and successive levels of managers cascading down below, eventuating to the frontline employees at the very bottom. This implies that there is more and more authority as you go from the bottom toward the apex at the top and that the people at the lowest level have almost no authority at all.

Carlzon simply inverted the triangle, placing the apex at the bottom and the frontline employees at the top. In doing so, he said that the job of managers is to make it possible for the front line to deliver the services that the customer expects. The manager is an enabler of employees. They are actually servants of employees, not their masters, when you look at it this way.

This is, to me, the essence of the project manager's role. Since you have very little authority anyway, consider that your job is to ensure that everyone in the project team has what he needs to do his job well. If you do, then most of your team will perform at appropriate levels.

> Since you have very little authority anyway, consider that your job is to ensure that all project team members have what they need to do their job well.

Leadership and Management

Finally, because the project manager's job is mostly about dealing with people, it is absolutely essential that you exercise leadership as well as management skills (see chapter 14). I have defined management as making an unsolicited contribution to the organization. The definition of leadership that seems to me to best express the meaning of the word is this (from *The Pyramid Climbers*): "Leadership is the art of getting others to want to do something that you believe should be done." The operative word in the definition is "want."

As mentioned previously, dictators get people to do things. Leaders get them to want to do things. There is a big difference.

As soon as the dictator turns his back, people quit working. When the leader turns her back, people continue working because they are working willingly. But, most important, the dictator can control only those people within his immediate range of sight.

Clearly, since he lacks authority, a project manager needs to exercise leadership. The leader can get people to perform without having to closely supervise them. And this is necessary in projects.

However, a project manager must also exercise management skills. In fact, the two sets of skills must be integrated into the job of project management because management deals with the administrative aspects of the job—budgets, schedules, logistics, and so on—while leadership gets people to perform at optimum levels. If you exercise one set of skills to the exclusion of the other, the outcome will be far less effective than if you integrate the two skill sets.

Do You Want to Be a Project Manager?

Project management is not for everyone. I emphasized earlier that it is not a technical job. It is about getting people to perform work that must be done to meet the objectives of the project. So, when I am asked what I consider to be the most important attributes for project managers to have, I always say that people skills are numbers one through three. Then, below that, comes everything else. If you can deal with people, you can either learn to do everything else or delegate it to someone who can do it. But being able to do everything else without being good at dealing with people just won't cut it.

Now the question is, do you really want to be a project manager? Do you like having responsibility with very limited authority? Do you enjoy working on impossible deadlines, with limited resources and unforgiving stakeholders? Are you, in other words, a bit masochistic? If you are, then you will love being a project manager.

If you are the boss of project managers, these are things you should consider in selecting people for the job. Not everyone is cut out for it.

KEY POINTS TO REMEMBER

- A project manager must understand the mission and vision of the organization first, see how the project they are managing meshes with the organization's mission, and then steer the project to ensure that the interests of the organization are met.
- The first skills a project manager needs are people skills.
- One of the biggest traps for project managers is to perform technical work in addition to managing the job because, when there is a conflict between performing the two, the project manager cannot neglect the management aspects.
- Instead of asking for authority, make decisions yourself, take action that is appropriate and does not violate policy, and then inform your boss what you have done.
- The project manager's job is to ensure that everyone in the project team has what he needs to do his job well.
- A project manager must exercise both leadership and management skills.

CHAPTER 3

PLANNING THE PROJECT

I n chapter 1, I talked about the high cost of project failures. Almost every study finds that failures are caused primarily by poor project management, especially the failure to plan properly. There are two barriers to good planning. The first is prevailing paradigms, and the second has to do with the nature of human beings.

A paradigm is a belief about what the world is like. You can tell what people believe by watching what they do because they always behave consistently with their deeply held beliefs. It is not necessarily what they say they believe but what they *really* believe that counts. Chris Argyris, in his book *Overcoming Organizational Defenses: Facilitating Organizational Learning* (Prentice Hall, 1990), has called these beliefs one's theory espoused as opposed to one's theory in practice. To illustrate, a fellow who attended my seminar on the tools of project management later told me that, upon returning to work, he immediately convened a meeting of his project team to prepare a plan. His boss called him out of the conference room.

"What are you doing?" asked the boss.

"Planning our project," explained the fellow.

"Oh, you don't have time for that nonsense," his boss told him. "Get them out of the conference room so they can get the job done!"

It is clear that his boss didn't believe in planning, which raises this question: Why did he send the fellow to a training program if he really didn't believe in what is taught? Go figure.

The second reason that people don't plan is that they find the activity painful. Some individuals, especially engineers and programmers, are concerned that they will be held to estimates of task durations that they have made using their best guesses. Because they have no historical data to draw on, this is all they can do. But they also know that such numbers are highly uncertain, and they are afraid that their failure to meet established targets will get them in trouble. As one of my engineers told me once, "You can't schedule creativity."

I replied that this may be true (but we must pretend we can because no one will fund the project unless we put down a time). Since then, I have changed my mind—you can schedule creativity, within limits. In fact, there is no better stimulus to creative thinking

[FIGURE 3-1]

TWO PAIN CURVES IN A PROJECT OVER TIME

than a tight deadline. If you give people forever, they simply mess around and don't produce anything.

Nevertheless, we find that when people are required to plan a project, they find the activity painful, and they resist the pain it causes. The net result is that they wind up on the Pain Curve 1 in figure 3-1. The total pain experienced is represented by the area under the curve.

In Curve 2 of the figure, there is a lot of pain early on, but it diminishes over time, and the total area under the curve is less than that under Curve 1.

The Absolute Imperative of Planning

If you consider the major function of managing, it is to ensure that the desired organization objectives are met. This is accomplished by exercising control over scarce resources. However, the word "control" has two connotations, and we must be careful which one we intend.

One meaning of the word is "power and domination." In management, this is sometimes called the command-and-control approach, which in its worst form degenerates into the use of fear and intimidation to get things done. This method works when people have no other desirable options for employment or are not free to leave (as in the military or a prison). However, in a robust economy, very few employees tolerate such management for long.

The second meaning of control—and the one I advocate for managers—is highlighted in the idea that control is exercised by comparing where you are to where you are supposed to be so that corrective action can be taken when deviation occurs. Notice that this is an information systems or guidance definition. Furthermore, note that two things are necessary for control to exist. First, you must have a plan that tells where you are supposed to be in the first place. If you have no plan, then you cannot possibly have control. I think we need to remind ourselves of this almost every day because it is so easy to forget when you are constantly being assaulted by demands to do this and that and a million other things.

> Control is exercised by comparing where you are to where you are supposed to be so that corrective action can be taken when deviation occurs.

Second, if you don't know where you are, you can't have control. Knowing where you are isn't as easy as it may seem, especially when doing knowledge work. For example, you say you expect to write ten thousand lines of code by today, and you've written eight thousand. Does that mean you're 80 percent of where you should be? Not necessarily. You may have found a more efficient way to write the code.

> No plan, no control!

In any event, the major point to remember is that you cannot have control unless you have a plan, so planning is not optional.

> "Predicting the future is easy. It's knowing what's going on now that's hard."
>
> —FRITZ R. S. DRESSLER

Another trap that causes people not to plan is to believe that they have no time to plan; they need to get the job done really fast! This is counterintuitive, but think about it: If you have forever to get something done, then you don't need a plan. It's when the deadline is tight that the plan becomes really important. As a simple example, imagine flying into Chicago and being late. You have a meeting across town in less than an hour. You've never been to Chicago, but when the rental car attendant asks if you need a map, you say, "I don't have time for a map. I've got to get to my meeting really fast!" Not very likely, is it?

Planning Defined

Planning is quite simply answering the questions shown in figure 3-2. They may be called the who/what/when/where/why/how-much/how-long questions that you learned if you ever studied interviewing methods. It is that simple. And it is that hard. I say "hard" because answering some of these questions requires a crystal ball—especially questions like, "How long will that take?" On tasks for which no history is available, this is a very hard question to answer. As my engineer said, "You can't schedule creativity."

[FIGURE 3-2]

PLANNING IS ANSWERING QUESTIONS

WHO WILL DO IT?

BY WHEN MUST IT BE DONE?

HOW MUCH WILL IT COST?

HOW SHOULD IT BE DONE?

WHAT MUST BE DONE?

HOW GOOD DOES IT HAVE TO BE?

Strategy, Tactics, and Logistics

To plan a project properly, you must attend to three kinds of activities that may have to be performed during the life of the job: strategy, tactics, and logistics.

Strategy refers to the overall method you will employ to do the job, sometimes referred to as a game plan. As I related in chapter 1, for thousands of years boats had been built with the keel down so that, when the boat is ready to be put into the water, it is already right side up. This method worked fine until the 1940s, when World War II placed tremendous pressure on shipyards to build military ships faster and ships were being built out of steel plates rather than wood. Shipbuilders quickly found that it was extremely difficult to weld in the keel area. From the outside, you had problems getting under the ship, and inside you had to stand on your head to weld.

Avondale Shipyard decided that it would be easier to build steel boats if ships were built upside down. The welding in the keel area now could be done from outside, standing above the ship, and to work on the inside the welders could stand upright. This strategy proved so effective that Avondale could build boats faster, cheaper, and of higher quality than its competitors, and the approach is still being used today.

Too often, planners choose a project strategy because "it has always been done that way" rather than because it is the best way to go. You should always ask yourself, "What would be the best way to go about this?" before you proceed to do detailed implementation planning.

Implementation Planning

Once you have decided to build boats upside down, you must work out all the details of how it will be done. Sometimes we say that we must be sure to dot all the "i's" and cross all the "t's." This is where you answer those who/what/when/where questions. In fact, it is *implementation planning* that many people think of when they talk about planning. However, a well-developed implementation plan for the wrong project strategy can only help you fail more efficiently.

Logistics

Military people can quickly tell you the benefit of attention to logistics. You can't fight a battle if people have no ammunition, food, clothing, or transportation. It is logistics that attends to these things. I once saw a project scheduling program (regrettably now defunct) that allowed construction managers to record when a certain quantity of bricks was delivered to their sites; the program then showed when they would run out, given a specific utilization rate, and would alert managers to schedule delivery of a new supply just before the existing stock was depleted.

I was also told about a road construction project in India that had very bad living conditions for the workers. The food was bad, sleeping conditions were poor, and the workers were suffering low morale. The project manager and his staff were all staying in a nice hotel in a nearby city. They finally realized the problem and moved to the site with the workers. Living conditions immediately improved, and so did worker morale and productivity. This is an example of the importance of the peripheral aspect of logistics.

Plan Ingredients

The following are the minimum ingredients that should be contained in a project plan. It is a good idea to keep these in a centralized project database. Initially, the electronic file will contain only the plan. As the project is managed, reports, changes, and other documents will be added so that when the project is completed, the file will contain a complete history of the project, which can be used by others as data for planning and managing their own projects.

Here are the items that make up the project plan:

- *Problem Statement.*
- *Project Mission Statement* (see chapter 5 for instructions on how to develop a mission statement).
- *Project Objectives* (see discussion in chapter 5).
- *Project Work Requirements.* This includes a list of all deliverables, such as reports, hardware, software, and so on. It is a good idea to have a deliverable at each major project milestone so that progress can be measured more easily.
- *Exit Criteria.* Each milestone should have criteria established that will be used to determine whether the preceding phase of work is actually finished. If no deliverable is provided at a milestone, exit criteria become very important.
- *End-Item Specifications to Be Met.* This means engineering specifications, architectural specs, building codes, government regulations, and so on.
- *Work Breakdown Structure (WBS).* This is an identification of all of the tasks that must be performed in order to achieve project objectives. A WBS is also a good graphic portrayal of project scope (see chapter 7).
- *Schedules* (both milestone and working schedules should be provided; see chapters 8 and 9).
- *Required Resources* (people, equipment, materials, and facilities). These must be specified in conjunction with the schedule (see chapters 8 and 9).
- *Control System* (see chapters 10, 11, and 12).
- *Major Contributors.* Use a linear responsibility chart (see chapter 7).
- *Risk Areas with Contingencies,* when possible (see chapters 5 and 6).

Sign-Off of the Plan

Once the plan has been prepared, it should be submitted to stakeholders for their signatures.

A stakeholder is anyone who has a vested interest in
the project. These include contributors, customers,
managers, and financial people.

Following are some comments about the meaning of signatures
and suggestions for handling the process:

- A *signature* means that the individual is committed to his
  contribution, agrees with the scope of work to be done, and
  accepts the specs as valid. A signature on the part of a contributor does not mean a guarantee of performance. It is a
  commitment. Because there are factors outside our control,
  few of us would like to guarantee our performance. However,
  most would be willing to make a commitment, meaning we
  promise to do our best to fulfill our obligations. If a signature
  is treated as a guarantee, either signers will refuse to sign, or
  they will sign without feeling really committed to the agree-
  ment. Neither response is desirable.
- The plan should be signed in a project plan review meeting,
  not by mail. Circulating copies for signature by mail seldom
  works, as people may be too busy to read in depth and may
  miss important points that would be brought out in a
  sign-off meeting.

The project plan should be reviewed and signed off
in a meeting—not through interoffice mail!

- People should be encouraged to "shoot holes in the plan"
  during the review meeting rather than waiting until problems develop later on. Naturally, this does not mean that
  they should nitpick the plan. The objective is to ensure that
  the plan is workable—that is all.

> **Encourage people to spot problems during the sign-off meeting, not later.**

Changing the Plan

It would be nice to think that a plan, once developed, would never change. However, that is unrealistic. No one has 20/20 foresight. Unforeseen problems are almost certain to arise. The important thing is to make changes in an orderly way, following a standard *change procedure*.

> **Make changes in an orderly way, following a standard *change procedure*.**

If no change control is exercised, the project may wind up over budget, behind schedule, and hopelessly inadequate, with no warning until it is too late. Here are suggestions for handling changes to the plan:

- Changes should be made only when a significant deviation occurs. A significant change is usually specified in terms of the percentage of tolerances relative to the original targets.
- Change control is necessary to protect everyone from the effects of scope creep—changes to the project that result in additional work. If changes in scope are not identified and managed properly, the project may come in considerably over budget and/or behind schedule.
- Causes of changes should be documented for reference in planning future projects. The causes should be factual, not blame-and-punishment statements.

"Any plan is bad which is not susceptible to change."
—BARTOLOMMNO DE SAN CONCORDIO (1475–1517)

A comprehensive process for managing project change is presented in chapter 11.

Suggestions for Effective Planning

Here are some ideas to help you plan effectively:

- *Plan to plan.* It is always difficult to get people together to develop a plan. The planning session itself should be planned, or it may turn into a totally disorganized meeting of the type that plagues many organizations. This means that an agenda must be prepared, the meeting should be time limited to the degree possible, and people should be kept on track. If someone goes off on a tangent, the meeting facilitator should get that person back on track as quickly as possible. There are many excellent guides to running meetings (e.g., *The Surprising Science of Meetings* by Steven G. Rogelberg [Oxford University Press, 2019]); the reader is referred to those.
- The people who must implement a plan should participate in preparing it. Otherwise, you risk having contributors who feel no sense of commitment to the plan; their estimates may be erroneous, and major tasks may be forgotten.

    Rule: The people who do the work should participate in developing the plan.

- The first rule of planning is to be prepared to replan. Unexpected obstacles will undoubtedly crop up and must be handled. This also means that you should not plan in too much detail if there is a likelihood that the plan will have to be changed, as this wastes time.

> **The first rule of planning is to be prepared to replan.**

- Because unexpected obstacles will crop up, always conduct a risk analysis to anticipate the most likely ones (see chapter 6). Develop Plan B just in case Plan A doesn't work. Why not just use Plan B in the first place? Because Plan A is better but has a few weaknesses. Plan B has weaknesses also, but they must be different from those in Plan A, or there is no use in considering Plan B a backup.

  The simple way to do a risk analysis is to ask, "What could go wrong?" This should be done for the schedule, work performance, and other parts of the project plan. Sometimes, simply identifying risks can help avert them, but if that cannot be done, at least you'll have a backup plan available. One caution: If you are dealing with very analytical people, they may go into analysis paralysis here. You are not trying to identify every possible risk—just those that are fairly likely.

> **Identify project risks and develop contingencies to deal with them if they occur.**

- Begin by looking at the purpose of doing whatever is to be done. Develop a problem statement. All actions in an organization should be taken to achieve a result, which is another way of saying, "solve a problem." Be careful here to identify what the end user really needs to solve the problem. Sometimes we see projects in which the team thinks a solution is right for the client, but that solution is never used, resulting in significant waste to the organization.

"Consider the little mouse, how sagacious an animal
it is which never entrusts its life to one hole only."
—PLAUTUS (254–184 BCE)

■ Use the work breakdown structure (discussed in chapter 7)
to divide the work into smaller chunks for which you can
develop accurate estimates for duration, cost, and resource
requirements.

PROJECT PLANNING STEPS

The basic planning steps are as follows. Note that some of these
topics are covered in the next chapter.

- Define the problem to be solved by the project.
- Develop a mission statement, followed by statements of major
  objectives.
- Develop a project strategy that will meet all project objectives.
- Write a scope statement to define project boundaries (what will
  and will not be done).
- Develop a work breakdown structure (WBS).
- Using the WBS, estimate activity durations, resource require-
  ments, and costs (as appropriate for your environment).
- Prepare the project master schedule and budget.
- Decide on the project organization structure—whether matrix
  or hierarchical (if you are free to choose).
- Create the project plan.
- Get all project stakeholders to sign off on the plan.

KEY POINTS TO REMEMBER

- If you have no plan, you have no control.
- The people who must execute a plan should participate in preparing it.
- Have the plan signed off in a meeting, not by sending it through the interoffice mail.
- Keep all project documentation in an electronic project file.
- Use exit criteria to determine when a milestone has actually been achieved.
- Require that changes to the project plan be approved before you make them.
- Risk management should be part of all project planning.
- A paradigm is a belief about what the world is like.
- Planning is answering the who/where/why/what/when/how/how-long/how-much questions.
- Logistics refers to supplying people with the materials and supplies they need to do their jobs.

EXERCISE

We have talked about strategy, tactics, and logistics.

Which must be decided first?

a. Strategy
b. Tactics
c. Logistics
d. Does not matter

What is the function of tactics?

When would you plan for logistics?

CHAPTER 4

INCORPORATING STAKEHOLDER MANAGEMENT IN THE PROJECT PLANNING PROCESS

As mentioned in chapter 3, a *stakeholder* is anyone who has a vested interest—in other words, who *holds* a *stake*—in the outcome of the project. This category may include contributors, customers, managers, and financial people. PMI defines a stakeholder as "an individual, group, or organization that may affect, be affected by, or perceive itself to be affected by a decision, activity, or outcome of a project, program, or portfolio" (*PMBOK® Guide*, PMI, 2021, p. 250). Regardless of how the role is defined, project stakeholders must be identified and then managed throughout the life of the project because they have a direct effect on whether your project will succeed or fail.

> *Stakeholder:* Anyone who has a vested interest in the outcome of a project.

Early in my career at Grumman Aerospace, I was part of a team of procurement specialists who were directed to create and implement a supplier performance rating system. It was a good team and we worked hard, but nobody was trained in project management. As a result, some planning activities were accomplished formally, as a process (scheduling, budget), and others were not—specifically, managing stakeholders. But we forgot to include an important group, Grumman's Texas office, in the creation of the new system. They were not happy. While business etiquette and decorum prevent one from printing their exact response, needless to say it was direct, and it would have been painful to do what was suggested. This delayed the project and caused a great deal of needless conflict. Had we done our job and identified our stakeholders from the beginning of the planning process, the project would have been completed on time and within budget. It was an unforced error that did not have to happen.

Prioritizing Stakeholders

Managing stakeholders does not have to be difficult, but it does take some effort. It begins with identifying the individual stakeholders, which you can do by asking three basic questions:

1. *Who benefits from the project?* Focus on the project deliverable and who will benefit from it. The deliverable could be any number of things, including a new internal process, software application, or new product to be marketed.
2. *Who contributes to the project?* Determine which individuals or groups you will be relying on to accomplish the project work. This could include project team members, the project sponsor, and subject matter experts outside the project team.
3. *Who is impacted by the project?* The project deliverable can impact others who do not necessarily benefit from it, such as the IT department updating software for buyers

or engineering supplying priority data for a new marketing campaign. These individuals and groups must be considered stakeholders because their work will be affected by the deliverable.

....

Managing stakeholders begins with identifying the individual stakeholders by asking three basic questions:

1. Who benefits from the project?
2. Who contributes to the project?
3. Who is impacted by the project?

....

You then must analyze how each of the stakeholders relates to your project. Some will be supportive; others will not. It is particularly important that "negative" stakeholders be prioritized and their concerns addressed (if possible). A negative stakeholder might be your best friend at work, but she needs the same resources required for your project for her own project. A negative stakeholder might also be a department manager who resists change— the change that your project deliverable will bring. There could be any number of reasons why a stakeholder does not have a positive attitude toward your project. Your job is to find out who they are and what is behind this attitude.

The stakeholder grid, shown in figure 4-1, is an excellent tool to help you manage stakeholders. Once they are identified, stakeholders can be analyzed as to their attitude (or support) toward your project and influence (or power) within the organization. Once these dynamics are determined, you can place them in the appropriate grid quadrant. Some of these stakeholders will literally be in your corner; others will not. Your response to and interaction with these stakeholders will depend upon which quadrant they occupy.

[FIGURE 4-1]
THE STAKEHOLDER GRID

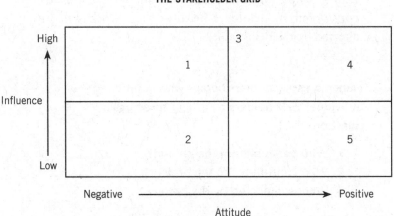

Those stakeholders with low influence or power do not demand much of your time or effort because their impact will be minimal. Those with high influence or power can be devastating if their attitude is negative, but their power can be leveraged if their attitude is positive. For example:

- *Person 2.* His attitude is negative toward the project, but his influence is low. Limited effort is required here, but I would keep him on my radar; he may get promoted.
- *Person 5.* Her attitude toward the project is positive, but her influence is low. This is good but not particularly helpful.
- *Persons 3 and 4.* These stakeholders have a positive attitude toward the project, and their influence is high. Here is an opportunity to leverage their influence to help persuade others.
- *Person 1.* Person 1 is dangerous because she has a negative attitude about your project and her influence is high. She can kill the project if she is not managed correctly. This may require a formal meeting, coffee in the morning, a nice lunch, or a couple of happy hour beverages. Your goal is to find out

what her objection to the project is and work to bring her into your corner.

With proper planning, there's no reason for a project manager to be blindsided. Front-load your effort, then invest time and work accordingly to make your project a success. In chapter 14, I cover the project manager as a leader. Here is where you put your leader hat on and work to persuade.

Engaging Key Stakeholders

Stakeholder engagement represents the project manager's effort, as you manage and execute the project, to involve stakeholders and understand stakeholder concerns. Some stakeholders are key to your project's success. You must have them engaged or involved for it to succeed. Some you may want to involve because of their expertise or institutional knowledge. Others you may want to involve because of the strength of their influence within the organization or among the participating parties.

> **Stakeholders are key to your project's success; they must be involved in order for it to succeed.**

In the *Project Management Body of Knowledge* (*PMBOK® Guide*, sixth edition, fig. 13-6), PMI has published a model for the Stakeholders Engagement Assessment Matrix (see figure 4-2). This matrix helps with the overall management of stakeholders by plotting current and desired levels of engagement. The engagement matrix acts as an effective complement to the stakeholder register, as it enables you to plot the desired engagement level for each stakeholder. You can then formulate and execute a plan to drive each of them toward the desired level of their engagement with the project.

[FIGURE 4-2]

THE STAKEHOLDERS ENGAGEMENT ASSESSMENT MATRIX

Stakeholder	Unaware	Resistant	Neutral	Supportive	Leading
Stakeholder 1	C			D	
Stakeholder 2			C	D	
Stakeholder 3				D C	

KEY:

Unaware. Unaware of project and potential impact.
Resistant. Aware of project and potential impacts and resistant to change.
Neutral. Aware of project yet neither supportive nor resistant.
Supportive. Aware of project and potential impacts and supportive to change.
Leading. Aware of project and potential impacts and actively engaged in ensuring the project is a success.
C = Current engagement
D = Desired engagement

In the figure, Stakeholder 1 is unaware, and you want him to be supportive. You have some work to do. Stakeholder 2 is neutral, and you want her to be supportive. Perhaps you have a short meeting or a cup of coffee and try to move her to support your project. Stakeholder 3 is already supportive. This is obviously good news, and he will require little or no effort moving forward. You can check periodically to make sure he remains happy.

Be proactive and maximize stakeholder involvement. Invest the time and effort necessary to create a Stakeholders Engagement Assessment Matrix. In the fog of the typical project environment, it is always useful to have a simple matrix to rely on. Oh yes, keep it current!

Stakeholder Alignment and Communication

Do all of your stakeholders agree with every element of your project as stated in the project charter? Probably not. Stakeholders are many and varied, and they are often affected differently by the project deliverable. They also have varying levels of technical expertise and product/project knowledge.

To get everyone moving in the same direction and thereby maximizing interaction, gauge their overall experience and project knowledge levels. In order to influence your stakeholders effectively, you must align your knowledge level with theirs, so you are speaking a common project language. Workplace learning expert Karen Feely cautions against the so-called Curse of Knowledge that affects many project managers. She suggests that you "remember that not everybody knows as much as you do about a topic. You need to speak to their levels of understanding."

To overcome this curse, Ms. Feely suggests that you focus on four distinct groups when aligning and communicating with your stakeholders (see figure 4-3).

[FIGURE 4-3]

AUDIENCE GUIDE TO KNOWLEDGE AND COMMUNICATION

Audience Guides	Knowledge Level	Communication
Project Manager	• Deeply knowledgeable about project/subject—knows technical terms, jargon, and acronyms.	• Acceptable to use jargon and acronyms and not explain terms.
Client SMEs and Client PM	• Fairly knowledgeable about project/subject. Some knowledge about project process but not all technical terms.	• Translate technical language into project language. • Include a glossary of project/technical terms.
Project Sponsors	• Have big picture. • Not focused on details. • Very limited to understanding of technical jargon.	• They are most concerned about hitting project goals and vision. • Less technical jargon and detail required.

Audience Guides	Knowledge Level	Communication
Everyone Else (End Users, etc.)	• Know how things currently work. • No real project knowledge.	• Translate terms. • Communicate vision and goals. • Avoid technical terms.

Most people communicate in their comfort zones. Project managers must plan and execute stakeholder communication in a focused and flexible process. The Curse of Knowledge may be lifted when you encounter a stakeholder with deep technical understanding of your project work, but she will still need to make herself understood by the others. Work with this stakeholder to make her an asset, not an impediment to project progress.

> Most people communicate in their comfort zone, so the project manager must plan and execute stakeholder communication in a focused and flexible process.

Managing Multicultural Stakeholders

Project managers will naturally develop an intuition for the dynamics of their working environments. This comes with the experience of managing within established organizational structures and interaction with individuals within defined workplace cultures. The organizational infrastructure will be self-evident and populated with familiar processes, rules, and regulations. The cultural environment of an organization can be more nuanced, however, and require some work by the project manager to measure the dynamics and drive effective stakeholder interaction.

Management Adjustments Based on the Stakeholder's Culture

Where am I now? This is a simple question that can be used to determine whether adjustments must be made in your approach to managing project stakeholders in different corporate environments. Are you leading individuals from other departments, facilities, locations, or countries? Do you understand their working cultures and how they differ from yours? Flex your style to get the most out of your team members and other stakeholders.

Back in 2008, I was teaching an MBA project management course for the City University of New York Graduate School. One of my students brought in a guest speaker (the CFO of a major global finance company) who spoke about organizational culture shock. She was a fascinating woman who recounted her experience at a previous company. There, if you were attending a 10:00 a.m. meeting, it meant you should arrive at least five minutes early, or you were late. In her current organization, 10:00 a.m. can mean five or ten minutes after ten, and then everybody will want to hear about her brother's new baby. She did not adjust quickly and eventually was approached by a colleague to help her amend her style.

The Five Cultural Dimensions

When interacting with stakeholders, their cultures should always be a consideration. In 1974, Dutch social psychologist Geert Hofstede conducted a study with a large pool of IBM employees worldwide. His study found that a society's value system is a combination of five key dimensions (see figure 4-4). These dimensions identify behavioral indicators within the working culture. The tendency of individuals to use a similar combination of these dimensions is what results in the formation of a unique culture. This can be a very useful tool for project managers when managing stakeholder culture.

[FIGURE 4-4]
THE FIVE CULTURAL DIMENSIONS

Dimension	Cultures Scoring Low	Cultures Scoring High
1. Power	Rely on consensus to make decisions.	Rely on hierarchical structures to make decisions.
2. Uncertainty Avoidance	Are comfortable with ambiguous or unknown situations.	Feel threatened by ambiguous or unknown situations. Prefer structure and predictability.
3. Individualism	Value the team above the individual.	Value autonomy. Put the individual's needs ahead of the team's.
4. Assertiveness	Tend to be more modest.	Tend to self-promote.
5. Time Perspective	Look to what provides immediate benefits.	Look to what will benefit the organization in the long run.

Understanding these dimensions will help you build trust. In a relationship with a stakeholder, absent trust is not a relationship. It is a time bomb. It is a risk waiting to become a reality.

When managing multicultural stakeholders, the trust factor becomes especially important. Growing up in the Grumman project environment, the cultural challenges were few. Everybody looked and acted alike; Grumman drew from a common resource pool. When I accepted the Global Practice Leader, Project Management position at AMA, the headquarters in New York City was staffed with employees from all over the world. One of my team members wanted to read my palm and tell my future, but I didn't want to know. I told her I had a risk management plan for that. The AMA culture presented me with an opportunity for tremendous personal growth but significant stakeholder management challenges. I eventually earned the trust of my stakeholders, but a proactive five-dimension approach would have been much more efficient.

Working with Remote, External Stakeholders

"Out of sight, out of mind." Most enduring sayings endure because they contain an element of truth. The distributed nature of our project teams and stakeholders requires a full-time effort (see chapter 14). Remote, external project stakeholders always present unique challenges. We are usually forced to meet and communicate with these stakeholders via Skype, Zoom, Teams, and other technology. Talk about relationship barriers!

Invest time and effort in one-on-one interaction. Get to know each other, and use the five dimensions as a tool. This can help mitigate or prevent initial distrust. More important, this will help you map your approach to work with remote, external stakeholders individually and collectively. The project manager as leader utilizes trust as an invaluable commodity. Using this strategy will help you build and hold trust *and* communicate more effectively.

> **Invest time and effort in one-on-one interaction when working with remote, external stakeholders.**

Uniting Stakeholders

Yes, we have all heard about the problem of trying to herd cats. Well, try uniting stakeholders from different cultures and backgrounds and managing them as a group throughout the life of a project. Think about your own project experiences. You have just completed phase III, and the operations manager has a *great* idea. You know that it is too late and that the impact of this idea on the project will be counterproductive, at the very least. The stakeholder grid in figure 4-1 shows that this stakeholder is highly influential. Here you must manage the disagreement. Don't be a complainer; be a persuader. Let logic and data help you with this and all disagreements with stakeholders. I often use the following four-step process when managing stakeholder disagreements:

- *Step 1.* Clarify your stakeholder's position *before* you take action. Make sure you understand his concerns first.
- *Step 2.* Describe the impact to the project that implementation of this new idea will have. This is often an *aha* moment for the stakeholder and can immediately diffuse the situation.
- *Step 3.* Alternative ideas can be persuasive if your stakeholder is firmly entrenched. Offer pros and cons of each idea.
- *Step 4.* Transition to negotiation. We all do it every day as we work on our projects. Negotiating with stakeholders is a fact of project life. The best-case scenario will front-load all negotiations early in the planning stage. Reality dictates their happening throughout the project life cycle. Before you negotiate:
  - Do your due diligence—plan.
  - Know what changes your project plan can and cannot absorb.
  - Manage scope creep by negotiating needed resources/time during the negotiation.
  - Win-win; find the common ground that makes sense for the stakeholder *and* the project.

Remember, stakeholders are there for a reason. You need them, and they need you for your project to be a success. Leverage their strengths and minimize their negative effects. Use common sense, and rely on some or all of the stakeholder management tools presented in this chapter. Identify those that make sense for you and your project, and you will find the road to on-time and under-budget completion much easier.

KEY POINTS TO REMEMBER

- A stakeholder is anyone who has a vested interest in the outcome of a project.
- Managing stakeholders begins with identifying the individual stakeholders by asking three basic questions: (1) Who benefits from the project? (2) Who contributes to the project? (3) Who is impacted by the project?
- Because stakeholders are key to a project's success, they must be engaged or involved in order for it to succeed.
- The cultural environment of an organization can be nuanced and thus require work by the project manager to measure the dynamics and to drive effective stakeholder interaction.
- Time and effort should be invested in one-on-one interaction with remote, external stakeholders.

CHAPTER 5

DEVELOPING A MISSION, VISION, GOALS, AND OBJECTIVES FOR THE PROJECT

B efore a project team does any work, it should spend time ensuring that it has a shared understanding of where it is going. The terms used to define that destination are "mission," "vision," "goals," and "objectives." And it is at this very early stage that projects tend to fail because everyone takes for granted that "we all know what the mission is."

Defining the Problem

Every project solves a problem of some kind, but people are inclined to skip over the definition of the problem. This is a big mistake. The way you define a problem determines how you will solve it, so it is critical that a proper definition be developed. For example, too often a problem is defined in terms of a solution. A person may say, "I have a problem. My car has quit, and I have no way to get to work. How am I going to get my car repaired because I have no money to do it?"

The problem has essentially been defined as, "How do I repair my car?" The actual problem, however, at its most fundamental level, is that the person has no way to get to work—or so he says. But could he ride the bus, go with a coworker, or ride a bike until he has the money to have the car repaired? It is true that having no money to repair the car is a problem, but it is important to distinguish between the basic, or core, problem and those at another level.

I once heard a sales manager berate a salesman, saying, "The company has spent a lot of money developing this new product, and none of you are selling it. If you don't get out there and sell this product, I'm going to find myself some salespeople who can sell!"

It is clear how he has defined the problem: he has a group of salespeople who can't sell. However, given that none of them can sell the product, I am sure he is wrong. There is something wrong with the product or market, or the competition is killing them. You are very unlikely to have all bad salespeople!

Nevertheless, this manager has defined the problem in terms of people, and that is the way it must be solved. Imagine that he replaces all of the salespeople. He will still have the same problem because he has not addressed the actual cause.

People sometimes define a problem as a goal. A goal in itself is not a problem. It is when there are obstacles that make it difficult to reach the goal that one has a problem. Given this definition of a problem, we can say that problem solving involves finding ways to deal with obstacles: they must be overcome, bypassed, or removed.

> **A goal in itself is not a problem. It is when there are obstacles that make it difficult to reach the goal that one has a problem.**

Confusion of Terms

Suppose a person tells you that she is taking a new job in a distant city, and she plans to move there. She immediately realizes that she must find a place to live. So she says, "I have a problem. I have to find a place to live."

You ask her what her mission is. "To find a place to live," she says.

And how about her vision? "To have a place to live," she answers, a little confused.

No wonder she is confused. All three statements sound alike! She needs to understand the difference between them if she is to solve this problem.

Remember, a problem is a gap. Suppose we were to ask her to tell us where she wants to be when her problem is solved. She would say, "I would have a place to live in the new city."

"And where are you now?" you ask.

"I have no place to live," she says.

Then the gap is between having a place and not having one. This can be stated simply as, "I have no place to live." And, indeed, this is the problem she is trying to solve.

But—would just anyplace be okay? Of course not. She doesn't want to live under a bridge, although homeless people sometimes do. So she can tell you if you ask her, "What kind of place are you looking for?"

"It needs to have three bedrooms, the house must be of a certain size, and I prefer a certain style," she says. This is her vision for the kind of place she wants to live in. That vision literally paints a picture in her mind, and, when she finds a place that comes close to that picture, she will have "arrived" at her destination. This is the function of vision: it defines "done."

Her mission, then, is to find a place that conforms to her vision. Another way to say this is that the mission of a project is always to achieve the vision. In doing so, it solves the stated problem. So you may want to diagram it, as shown in figure 5-1. Note that the vision has been spelled out as a list of things she must have, along with some that she wants to have and a few that would be nice to have if she could get them.

[FIGURE 5-1]

CHEVRON SHOWING MISSION, VISION, AND PROBLEM STATEMENT

Problem: I have no place to live.		
MUSTS	WANTS	NICE
3 bedrooms 2,500 sq. ft. 2-car garage 1-acre lot large family room	room for home office basement	fireplace in family room

Mission:
To find a place that meets all musts and as many of the others as possible.

The Real World

Okay, now we know the differences between the mission, vision, and problem, but in the real world you never get them in this order. Your boss or project sponsor will say, "Here is your mission," without any mention of a problem statement. It is possible that some discussion of the sponsor's vision of the end result will take place, but even that may be fairly sketchy. So the first order of business for a project team is to develop these into a form that everyone will accept.

The major "political" problem you may encounter is that the sponsor will undoubtedly have given you a mission that is based on his definition of the problem to be solved. Sometimes his definition will be incorrect, and you will have to confront this. Otherwise, you will spend a lot of the organization's money, only to find that you have developed the right solution to the wrong problem.

The Real Mission of Every Project

I said earlier that the mission is always to achieve the vision. However, I should add that the vision you are trying to achieve is the one the customer holds. Another way to say this is that you are trying to satisfy the customer's needs. That is the primary objective. Your motive may be to make a profit in the process, but the mission is always to meet the needs of the customer. That means, of course, that you must know what those needs are, and sometimes this isn't easy because even the customer isn't clear about them. So you have to translate or interpret as best you can. Your best safeguard is to keep the customer involved in the project from concept to completion so that there is a constant check on whether what you are doing will achieve the desired result.

The mission of the project can be written by answering two questions:

1. What are we going to do?
2. For whom are we going to do it?

It is also important to state how you will go about meeting those customer needs, but this should not be part of the mission statement itself. The mission statement defines *what* you are doing; *how* you are going to do it is project strategy and should be dealt with separately.

Developing Project Objectives

Once a mission statement has been developed, you can write your project objectives. Note that objectives are much more specific than the mission statement itself and define results that must be achieved in order for the overall mission to be accomplished. Also, an objective defines the desired end result.

> **Goal setting has traditionally been based on past performance. This practice has tended to perpetuate the sins of the past.**

I may want to finish this chapter by ten o'clock this morning. That is my desired outcome or result—my objective. The way in which I achieve that objective is to perform a number of tasks. These might include typing text into my computer, reviewing some other literature on the topic about which I am writing, calling a colleague to ask a question for clarification, and printing out the chapter, proofing it, and entering some revisions into my computer.

> **An *objective* specifies a desired end result to be achieved. A *task* is an activity performed to achieve that result. An objective is usually a noun, whereas a task is a verb.**

The following acronym may help you remember the essential qualities that a statement of objectives must have. We say that an objective must be SMART, with each letter standing for a condition as follows:

Specific
Measurable
Attainable
Realistic
Time limited

Dr. W. Edwards Deming has raised some serious questions about the advisability of trying to quantify goals and objectives. He argued that there is no point in setting quotas for a manufacturing process to reach. If the system is stable, he argued, then there is no need to specify a goal, since you will get whatever the system can produce. A goal beyond the capability of the system can't be achieved.

On the other hand, according to Deming, if the system is not stable (in the statistical sense of the word), then again there is no need to specify a quota, since there is no way to know what the capability of the system is.

In project work, we may know the capability of a person by looking at her past performance, but, unless you have a large number of samples, you have no way of knowing exactly what the person can do, since there is always variability in people's performance. Furthermore, it does no good to base a quota on what someone else has done. The quota must be valid for the person who is going to do the job this time.

We all know that some people are capable of more output than others. So defining the measurement and attainability aspects of a goal or objective setting is very difficult. I go into this more in chapter 6 when I discuss time estimating.

I have found the following two questions to be useful both in setting objectives and in monitoring progress toward those objectives:

1. *What is our desired outcome?* This is called the outcome frame. It helps keep you focused on the result you are trying to achieve, rather than on the effort being expended to get there.
2. *How will we know when we achieve it?* I call this the evidence question. This question is very useful for establishing exit criteria for objectives that cannot be quantified.

What follows are a couple of examples of objectives:

- Our objective is to develop a one-minute commercial to solicit contributions to WXYZ to air on local TV stations by June 5, 2023.
- Our objective is to raise $600,000 in funds from local viewers by September 18, 2023.

The Nature of Objectives

Note that these examples of objectives do not say how they will be achieved. I consider an objective to be a statement that tells me what result is to be achieved. The "how" is problem solving, and I prefer to keep that open so that solutions can be brainstormed later. If the approach is written into the objective statement, it may lock a team into a method that is not really best for the project.

Assessing Project Risks

Once you have established your objectives, you can develop plans for how to achieve them. Unfortunately, the best plans sometimes don't work. One safeguard in managing projects is to think about the risks ahead that could sink the job. This can be done for critical objectives and for other parts of the plan.

The simplest way to conduct a risk analysis is to ask, "What could go wrong?" or "What could keep us from achieving our objective?" It is usually best to list the risks first, then think about contingencies for dealing with them. One way to look at risk is to divide a flip chart page in half, have the group brainstorm the risks, which you write down on the left side of the page, and then go back and list the contingencies—things you can do to manage the risks if they do materialize. An example of a risk analysis for a photography project is shown in figure 5-2.

It is helpful to assess risks of failure of the following:

- The schedule
- The budget
- Project quality
- Customer satisfaction

[FIGURE 5-2]

RISK ANALYSIS EXAMPLE

What could go wrong?	Contingency
1. Exposure wrong	Bracket the exposure
2. Shots unacceptable	Take extra photos
3. Film lost or damaged	Hand-carry to client
4. Weather delays	Allow extra time

One benefit of doing a risk analysis in this manner is that it may help you avert some risks. When you cannot avert a risk, you will at least have a backup plan. Unexpected risks can throw a project into a tailspin.

I mentioned this point previously, but it bears repeating: you are not trying to identify every possible risk, just some of the more likely ones. This point should be made to team members who are highly analytical or who perhaps have a tendency to be negative in general. Also, risk analysis always has a positive thrust—that is, you are asking, "If it happens, what will we do about it?" You don't want people to say, "Ain't it awful!"

Risk analysis should not lead to analysis paralysis!

In chapter 6, I present detailed tools and techniques to address risk management in the project environment.

KEY POINTS TO REMEMBER

- The way a problem is defined determines how you will solve it.
- A problem is a gap between where you are and where you want to be, with obstacles making it hard to reach the goal. A goal by itself is not a problem. Obstacles must exist for there to be a problem.
- Vision is what the final result will "look like." It defines "done."
- The mission is to achieve the vision. It answers the two questions "What are we going to do?" and "For whom are we going to do it?"
- Objectives should be SMART.
- You can identify risks by asking, "What could go wrong?"

EXERCISE

Choose a project that you are going to do or perhaps have just started. Answer the questions that follow to the best of your ability. If you need to confer with others to answer some of them, fine. Remember, the people who have to follow the plan should participate in preparing it.

- ▶ What are you trying to achieve with the project? What need does it satisfy for your customer? Who exactly is actually going to use the finished project deliverable(s)? (That is, who is your real customer?) What will distinguish your deliverable from those already available to the customer?

▶ Write a problem statement on the basis of your answers to the first question. What is the gap between where you are now and where you want to be? What obstacles prevent easy movement to close the gap?

▶ Write a mission statement, answering the two basic questions:
1. "What are we going to do?"
2. "For whom are we going to do it?"

Talk to your customer about these issues. Do not present your written statements to her. Instead, see whether you can get confirmation by asking open-ended questions. If you can't, you may have to revise what you have written.

CHAPTER 6

CREATING THE PROJECT RISK AND COMMUNICATION PLANS

As mentioned in chapter 1, risk management is the systematic process of identifying, analyzing, and responding to project risk. *Systematic* is a key word here, as many project managers attempt to deal with risks on an informal basis with little or no prior planning. Any project manager who operates in this manner is inviting failure, if not disaster. These are strong words but appropriate for an important topic. A formal, comprehensive project risk plan allows the project manager to be proactive regarding the innumerable things that can and do go wrong with a project. Without this plan, you are forced to manage reactively when things go wrong—easily the most expensive approach. A systematic process adds discipline and efficiency when creating the plan. At the end of chapter 5, a high-level overview of the risk process was presented. Here we present a comprehensive approach to project risk management.

■ ■ ■

A formal, comprehensive project risk plan allows the project manager to be proactive regarding the innumerable things that can and do go wrong with a project.

Defining Project Risk Management

Project risk management begins early in the life cycle. A clear understanding of the risks that the project faces must be established. The sources of project risk are almost limitless, emphasizing the need for a well-thought-out, detailed plan. Typical examples include the loss of a key team member, weather emergencies, technical failures, and poor suppliers.

Many project managers wait too long to assess risk factors and delay creating a risk management plan because they assume they don't know enough yet, that there are too many unknowns. This is a common trap that you should try to avoid. During the initiation phase of the project life cycle, an initial high-level assessment ought to be conducted. You and your team members should take a strategic approach to "what can go wrong" and begin laying the foundation for the detailed plan to follow. Without this foundation, projects often experience the negative impact of risks that become reality, risks that might have been prevented or mitigated through contingency planning. This is *reactive* behavior, and you must live in the *proactive* world to be successful as a project manager. Potential opportunities are sometimes referred to as "positive risks," where the project manager strives to optimize the positive impact on project objectives.

The new *PMBOK® Guide* (7, p. 248) describes a risk management plan as "a component of the project, program, or portfolio management plan that describes how risk management activities will be structured and performed." *The management of project risks is a process.* By definition, a process can be considered a formal, controlled undertaking with little or no variation. When applied to processes, variation often equals inefficiency. It is important for you to manage risks formally by applying an agreed-upon process to establish the risk management plan. Given the realities and variables of the typical project environment, a certain amount of flexibility is appropriate. As you gain experience in managing risks, an intuitive feel for flexibility will develop depending upon style and the length, width, depth, and breadth of the projects.

A project risk management plan is "a component of the project, program, or portfolio management plan that describes how risk management activities will be structured and performed."

The Six-Step Process for a Project Risk Plan

The Six-Step Process is a common and practical approach to establishing the project risk plan. This process should not be created in a vacuum and typically involves a great deal of research and collaboration with the project team.

Step 1: Make a List

Brainstorm. Making a list of potential risks to the project should not be an analysis but a formal brainstorming session, when all ideas are captured. Steps 2 and 3 of the process allow for a vetting of these ideas. It is important that the entire team get involved in identifying threats and highlighting what can go wrong. Some project managers make the mistake of trying to accomplish this on their own in order to allow team members to complete other tasks. This is shortsighted and a bad idea. This initial step of the process must be collaborative and involve the individuals who are experts at the portions of the project work for which they are responsible. Leverage the intellectual capital (smarts) that is your team. If one or more members are left out, it is likely that some risks will remain unidentified and pose a threat to project success. Remember, involve everyone—a procurement specialist will not be helpful in identifying potential software development problems, and vice versa.

Step 1: Make a list.

When you work with the support of an informal team, you will need to be disciplined and realize that a certain amount of research is necessary before moving forward. This may include phone calls, emails, videoconferencing, or office visits—whatever it takes to elicit the information you need. You typically start with the informal team members or contributors to the project and initiate a dialogue as to what might go wrong. Usually, these discussions identify other ancillary individuals who should be contacted. Functional department managers can be very helpful in these circumstances, either assisting directly or identifying others in their department who can.

In either case, you should take a holistic approach to establishing the list, as all types of risks will need to be identified and dealt with accordingly.

Steps 2 and 3: Determine the Probability of Risk Occurrence and Negative Impact

I am combining Steps 2 and 3 because they are the prioritization factors. They assist you in vetting the list of risks. These two steps allow you to prioritize all identified threats to the project and help you determine how much time, effort, staff, and money should be devoted to preventing or mitigating each. Again, this must be accomplished not in a vacuum but with full input from team members and subject matter experts (SMEs).

Steps 2 and 3: Determine the probability of risk occurrence and negative impact.

How probable is it that each risk will become a reality? This question needs to be asked and answered. It is often sufficient to use a High-Medium-Low (HML) scale and apply it to the list of brainstormed risks. If a risk is considered highly probable, it receives an H; if the probability is medium, it receives an M; and if the probability is low, it receives an L. These labels should not be applied arbitrarily, emphasizing the need for team collaboration or research and analysis by the project manager.

If the risk becomes a reality, how badly will it damage the project? This is the next question that needs to be asked and answered. All aspects of the project should be considered when rating the negative impact of any risk. If the risk becomes reality, how will it affect the budget, schedule, resource utilization, scope of work, and so on? The output of Steps 2 and 3 results in a list of potential risks with corresponding values for Probability and Negative Impact:

Risk	Probability	Negative Impact
A	M	L
B	M	M
C	L	L
D	H	H

Given the assessment of Risks A through D in the table, it is clear that you should focus most of your efforts on mitigating Risk D and that very little attention should be paid to Risk C. Please remember that you could be wrong (unfortunately, I needed to be reminded of this as a young project manager). Just because you label a risk Low probability and Low impact does not guarantee that it will be, so leave it on your radar screen.

For those who prefer metrics, a simple number-based scale can be applied. As you rate probability and impact, you assign a value to each risk. The probability scale can be based on a range of 1 through 10, with 1 representing unlikely and 10 being very likely. Negative impact can be represented by the same scale or by budgetary impact:

Risk	Probability		$ Impact		Total
A	3	×	1K	=	3K
B	7	×	1K	=	7K
C	2	×	14K	=	28K
D	5	×	3K	=	15K

According to this analysis, Risk C will demand most of this project team's attention because of its relative value of 28K. It should be noted that the same method can be used to focus on schedule impact or even resource utilization.

Step 4: Prevent or Mitigate the Risk

Some risks can be prevented; others can only be mitigated. Earthquakes or the retirement of an important stakeholder, for instance, cannot be prevented. Some risks can and should be prevented in Step 4. If a risk has been identified and you have the ability to prevent its occurrence, do so. Proactivity is the project manager's best friend. Kill the risk before it has a chance to grow and flourish, and you won't have to deal with it again.

....
Step 4: Prevent or mitigate the risk.
....

For example, if a vendor or supplier is targeted for your project and one of your team members has had previous dealings with the company and was not impressed, he will inform you that the supplier's material deliveries are frequently late and often rejected. Assuming that the supplier is not a sole source (your only choice), you can prevent the risk by finding an alternate supplier that is more reliable.

For those risks that cannot be prevented, an attempt should be made to mitigate or lessen the probability and/or impact should they occur. Using the example of the unreliable supplier, if you must use that company, you can create concrete steps to proactively expedite the delivery of the material, thereby mitigating the impact of the risk. If management threatens to deprioritize your project, you can lobby on your project's behalf, mitigating the chances that this will occur.

Step 5: Consider Contingencies

Preventive measures are those steps taken before the risk becomes reality. Contingencies represent the specific actions that will be taken if the risk occurs. Here, you answer the question "If the risk becomes reality, what will we do?"

....

Step 5: Consider contingencies.

....

For example, if acceptance testing for a supplier's widgets has been identified as medium to high risk and a test failure occurs, an appropriate contingency might be to supply engineering support at the vendor's expense. Another contingency might be to switch to another predetermined vendor if he has widgets in stock.

Contingencies are directly linked to the prioritization factors introduced in Steps 2 and 3. If the risk is a high priority (high probability, high negative impact), you will want to identify multiple contingencies. Since there is a good chance that the risk will occur and that when it does, it will hurt the project, you want to be covered. If the risk falls in the middle range of the prioritization scale, you should establish at least one contingency. Those risks that fall in the lower level should not require much attention; it is best to invest your efforts elsewhere. When establishing your contingencies, be careful of the very low probability, very high impact risk. These tend to be totally ignored because of the low probability, but they can and sometimes do bring projects down.

Step 6: Establish the Trigger Point

The *trigger point* is often the most important element of the project risk plan. There is a direct relationship between the trigger point and the contingencies. True to its name, the trigger point is the point at which the risk becomes enough of a reality that the project manager needs to trigger the contingency. It is a judgment call meant to maximize the value of the predetermined contingency by implementing it at the optimal time. Trigger too soon, and you will probably spend time, effort, or money for no good reason. Trigger too late, and you may end up experiencing the full impact of the occurrence, with little value added by implementing the contingency. Let's return to our example.

If a usually reliable supplier has experienced labor issues and has shut down because of a strike, perhaps your contingency plan has identified suppliers B and C as alternatives. Each has widgets in stock and has quoted a lead time of two calendar weeks for prep and delivery. If the required delivery date is February 15, your trigger should include the two-week lead time plus a few days' buffer. An appropriate trigger point here would be January 28. If the contingency affects a task or tasks on the critical path (see chapter 8), additional buffer days should be considered.

The trigger should be a specific point in time or a defined range of time. Most project managers consider this to be the trickiest part of the project risk plan, but it is well worth the effort. Often, in my role as consultant, I come across well-thought-out plans that were wasted due to untimely or nonexistent contingency implementation. The trigger point is a best practice for project managers that will improve the efficacy of the entire plan.

Establishing Reserves

The most comprehensive risk plan can be compromised if you realize that you do not have the time or means to take appropriate action. *Establishing reserves* enables you to leverage the plan to its fullest potential. The best-laid plans are impotent without the time and/or budget to allow for effective implementation. As a result, you need to establish contingency and management reserves.

> The most comprehensive risk plan can be compromised if you realize that you do not have the time or means to take appropriate action.

Contingency reserves are designated amounts of time and/or budget to account for risks to the project that have been identified and actively accepted. They are created to cover *known* risks to the project. There is a direct relationship between contingency reserves and the previously discussed Six-Step Process (or a similar approach). Once the process is complete, you should estimate the required reserves to cover the risks that have been identified and accepted.

For example, if your project team has identified the loss of a key team member to retirement as a high-priority risk (probability and impact), contingency actions will require the hiring of a replacement from outside the organization. The cost and schedule impact of the hiring process and team member assimilation must be estimated and added to the contingency reserve.

Management reserves are designated amounts of time and/or budget included in your plan to account for risks to the project that cannot be predicted. Sometimes you don't know what you don't know. Management reserves are created to cover *unknown* risks to the project. For example, if the current project involves a high percentage of research and development, and an analysis of past similar projects using actuals (historical data) indicates an average budgetary overrun of 10 percent, this 10 percent is not attributed to any particular risk event. However, it should trigger the need for a 10 percent increase to the overall project budget as a management reserve.

Managing Multiproject Risks

Many, if not most, project managers find themselves leading more than one project. The multiproject manager confronts unique issues not normally encountered when managing a single project. In the multiproject world, many projects overlap or experience direct dependencies with other projects, similar to those in a typical network diagram (see chapters 8 and 9).

Two perspectives are required here. First, you must focus on the individual projects and the associated risks for each. Then, you must assess your entire portfolio and determine the nature of the relationship among these projects. Your *portfolio* is the sum of all projects under your purview. The relationship among these projects may vary widely.

A *program* typically involves multiple projects working toward the completion of a single deliverable. These projects must all be properly integrated toward this end. In the portfolio environment, you must identify where the projects coincide or overlap with regard to any project work. You then determine what might go wrong in these areas where the projects "touch."

A *program* typically involves multiple projects working toward the completion of a single deliverable.

The same is done in the program environment, where project relationships are usually more clearly defined. For example, track and field includes events involving four runners who must pass a baton from one to the other. The fastest team does not always win because the baton may not be handed off smoothly, or it may even be dropped. Many projects will have direct predecessor–successor relationships (one must be completed before the next can begin) in the program world. To promote a smooth transition from one project to the next, you must focus on this "baton" handoff. The multiproject risk plan focuses on just these events.

Coordination Points

In either case, the areas where the projects touch are called *coordination points*. You need to identify these points, after which a standard multiproject risk plan can be created. It is important to emphasize that the Six-Step focus here must be on the coordination points exclusively. In reality, you focus on creating a risk plan for each project individually to manage intraproject risks and then turn your attention to the coordination points and perform the same process to manage interproject risks. The portfolio or program risk plan is meant to supplement and enhance the individual risk plan in the multiproject environment.

Risk Matrix

A useful tool when managing many risks across projects is the standard *risk matrix*, as shown in figure 6-1. The risk matrix will help you plot your risks in quadrants according to probability and negative impact.

Once the threats have been plotted onto the risk matrix, an H-M-L prioritization can be applied where the highest-priority risks are positioned toward the upper right corner and lower priority ones toward the lower left. You can then color code individual risks as they apply to each project. In the fog of the portfolio or program management world, this can prove to be a very effective approach.

[FIGURE 6-1]

RISK MATRIX

Risk Register

The *risk register* is a useful tool in managing actions taken regarding accepted risks to the project, as shown in figure 6-2.

The risk register, the last ingredient of the project risk plan, is a living, breathing dynamic tool that can help you to track risk status as your project matures through the life cycle. The risk register also helps you identify ownership of contingency implementation, outcomes of actions taken, and active and inactive risks.

[FIGURE 6-2]

RISK REGISTER

ID	Risk	Outcome/Response	Owner	P	I	Active

P = Probability   I = Imapct

If a thorough risk analysis is not developed, you and your team will live in the reactive world, putting out fires throughout the project life cycle. This is easily the most expensive way to operate in terms of time, effort, and money, and it will jeopardize the success of any project. You must invest yourself early by adding this crucial element to your overall project plan.

The Communication Plan

When leading my project management seminars, I ask participants to identify challenges they encounter as they manage their projects. Communication, or the lack thereof, is the challenge highlighted most often, by far. It is good that most project managers realize how important effective communication is to project success, but it is equally frustrating to observe how few project managers take concrete steps to improve it.

Let's start with email. Yes, we still have meetings (virtual or otherwise), call our stakeholders on the phone, or personally visit our team members. But email still dominates the majority of project communication today. It's been around awhile, so I have gone with an email evolution that facilitates instant, worldwide (or across-the-hall) interaction. Email gives us the ability to prioritize responses and create a thread or "paper" trail, if necessary. These are good things, but I have observed that we have not fully grasped the technology and maximized its potential.

Have you ever received a five-page email of endless paragraphs? Some emails resemble a novel that should be dedicated to a loved one. Conversely, the three-bullet email can leave the recipient wondering what was left out. I call this the Wild West scenario of communication. There are no rules, laws, or guidelines. Project email communication is left to the whim and style of those communicating. This sounds like "winging it," and that does not work in a project environment constrained by scope, schedule, and budget.

Create an email protocol. Be proactive and determine who communicates with whom and when. Identify which emails should go to what stakeholders. Establish a guideline for *cc* emails. Have you ever returned from vacation only to face five hundred *cc* emails, with most having nothing to do with you or your project work? Not only is it drudgery to go through those emails, but it is a real time waster. Reach out to your team and include them as you create the email protocol. You will improve communication efficiency and enjoy buy-in from the team.

Here are some tips for project managers and teams when using email:

- Send the email only to those who need to know.
- Proofread the email before sending it; use spellcheck.
- Use the subject line to set the tone of the message.
- Create an email protocol and use it.
- If you are angry . . . wait a while before sending it.
- Do not write a novel; be succinct.
- Be succinct, but include all necessary information.
- Do not use email to avoid people.
- If the information is sensitive, consider a face-to-face meeting.

The project communication plan should include an email protocol and much more. Plan how you will communicate effectively as your project matures. Treat the act of communicating as formally as you do your WBS or project charter. Project managers work in a constrained, demanding environment where good is often not good enough. Project managers and team members must predetermine how stakeholders should interact to achieve maximum efficiency as they move through the project life cycle.

Here are some questions that should be asked and answered when creating the project communication plan:

- *What* are you trying to communicate?
- *When* must it be done (end of year, etc.)?
- *How* will the communication be accomplished (email, formal letter with original signature, meeting)?
- *How often* must the communication occur?
- *Who* owns the communication (makes sure that it happens)?
- *To whom* is the communication addressed?

Once you have answered these questions, you are ready to construct your communication plan (see a sample communication plan in figure 6-3).

[FIGURE 6-3]

COMMUNICATION PLAN

ID	Description	Owner	Medium	Frequency	To Whom
1	Management status report	Nicolle	Meeting	Monthly	Sponsor
2	Team member status collection	Kyle	One-on-one	Bi-weekly	PM
3	Detailed project plan	Sue	Share drive	On-demand	Requester

Some of the best project managers I have known and observed—smart, hardworking, software wizards—are not always successful because they fail to plan and execute project communication formally. They do not construct this plan. Make sure you do!

KEY POINTS TO REMEMBER

▶ Project risk management should begin early in the process and continue through the life cycle. A key to success in dealing with risk is to start early and lay the foundation for risk management; be proactive, not reactive; manage risks formally with a *process*; and be flexible.

- The Six-Step Process to establishing a project risk plan includes making a list of potential risks, determining the probability of risk occurrence, determining its negative impact, preventing or mitigating the risk, considering contingencies, and establishing trigger points for activating contingencies.
- Establishing contingency and management reserves enables you to leverage your project risk plan to its fullest potential.
- Coordination points must be identified and analyzed in the multiproject risk environment.
- A standard risk matrix is a useful tool when managing many risks across projects.
- The risk register can be an effective tool for organizing and prioritizing threats to the project.
- Create an email protocol; include your team for buy-in.
- Develop your project communication plan; it is as important as any other project process.

EXERCISE

Choose one of your current or recent projects, and practice the Six-Step Process. Make a list of potential risks to the project and prioritize each, utilizing H-M-L or a simple metric-based scale. Pick any three risks and establish:

- Preventive measures
- Contingencies
- Trigger points

Two or three bullet points for each should suffice.

CHAPTER 7

USING THE WORK BREAKDOWN STRUCTURE TO PLAN A PROJECT

I n a previous chapter, I said that planning answers the questions "What must be done?" "How long will it take?" and "How much will it cost?" Planning the *what* is vital; projects frequently fail because a significant part of the work is forgotten. In addition, once tasks have been identified, the time and resource requirements must be determined. This is called *estimating*.

A major problem in project planning is determining how long tasks will take and what it will cost to do them. Inaccurate estimates are a leading cause of project failures, and missed cost targets are a common cause of stress and recrimination in project management.

The most useful tool for accomplishing all of these tasks is the *work breakdown structure* (*WBS*). The idea behind the WBS is simple: You can subdivide a complicated task into smaller tasks until you reach a level that cannot be further subdivided. At that point, it is usually easier to estimate how long the small task will take and how much it will cost to perform than it would have been to estimate these factors at the higher levels.

Nevertheless, it is still not easy to estimate task durations for activities that have never been performed before. Because this is the typical situation in engineering hardware and software development projects, we might expect many of these estimates to be in error, and this seems to be demonstrated by experience. Still, the work breakdown structure makes it easier to estimate knowledge tasks than any other tool we have.

A Simple Example

As an example, if I want to clean a room (see figure 7-1), I might begin by picking up clothes, toys, and other things that have been dropped on the floor. I could use a vacuum cleaner to get dirt out of the carpet. I might wash the windows and wipe down the walls, then dust the furniture. All of these activities are *subtasks* performed to clean the room.

[FIGURE 7-1]

WBS DIAGRAM TO CLEAN A ROOM

As for vacuuming the room, I might have to get the vacuum cleaner out of the closet, connect the hose, plug it in, adjust the settings, push the vacuum cleaner around the room, and put the machine back in the closet. These are still smaller tasks to be performed in accomplishing the subtask called *vacuuming*. The diagram in figure 7-1 shows how this might be portrayed in WBS format.

Note that we do not worry about the sequence in which work is performed when we do a WBS. That will be worked out when we develop a schedule. However, you will probably find yourself thinking sequentially, as it seems to be human nature to do so. The main idea of doing a WBS is to capture all of the tasks. So if you find yourself and other members of your team thinking sequentially, don't be too concerned, but don't get hung up on trying to diagram the sequence, or you will slow down the process of task identification.

A work breakdown structure *does not show the sequence in which work is performed!* Such sequencing is determined when a schedule is *developed.*

The typical WBS has three to six levels, and these can be named as shown in figure 7-2. It is, of course, possible to have projects that require a lot more levels. Twenty levels is considered to be the upper limit, and that is a huge project. Note that Level 1 is called the *program* level. The difference between a program and a project is just one of degree.

An example of a program is the development of an airplane. The WBS for the program might be drawn as shown in figure 7-3. Notice that the engine, wing, and avionics are large enough jobs to be called projects in their own right. In fact, the program manager's job is to make sure that the projects are all properly integrated. The engine mounts on the wing, so, somewhere in the

[FIGURE 7-2]
WBS LEVEL NAMES

1. Program
2. Project
3. Task
4. Subtask
5. Work Package
6. Level of Effort

structure to develop the engine, there will be an activity called Design Wing Mounts. And for the wing, there will be an activity called Design Engine Mounts. If these are not coordinated properly, you will wind up with an engine that won't mount on the wing. The job of coordinating these is called *system integration*.

[FIGURE 7-3]
PARTIAL WBS

Guidelines for Developing the WBS

One important question in constructing a WBS is, "When do you stop breaking down the work?" The general guideline is that you stop when you reach a point where either you can estimate time and cost to the desired degree of accuracy or the work will take an amount of time equal to the smallest units you want to schedule. If, for instance, you want to schedule to the nearest day, you break down the work to the point where tasks take about a day to perform. If you are going to schedule to the nearest hour, then you stop when task durations are in that range.

> **Stop breaking down work when you reach a low enough level to do an estimate of the desired accuracy.**

Remember the rule that the people who must do the work should participate in planning it? That applies here. Usually a core group identifies top-level parts of the WBS; those parts are further refined by other members of the team and then integrated to obtain the entire WBS.

One important point: The WBS should be developed before the schedule. In fact, the WBS is the device that ties the entire project together. It allows the manager to assign resources and to estimate time and cost and shows the scope of the job in graphic form. Later, as the project is tracked, the work can be identified as falling in a particular box in the WBS.

> **The WBS should always be developed before the schedule is worked out but without trying to identify the sequence of activities.**

Today, there are many project software packages that will print a WBS after schedule data have been entered. That is a nice feature, since it gives a graphically attractive WBS, but the rough drawing should be made before you use the scheduling software. The reason is quite simple: until everyone has agreed that all tasks have been identified, it is misleading to develop a schedule. You cannot be sure that the critical path identified by a partial schedule will be the same for the full schedule.

There are a number of approaches to developing the WBS. Ideally, you proceed top-down, following development of a good problem statement and mission statement. As I have mentioned, however, the mind does not always operate in such a nice, linear fashion; as you develop the WBS, you may sometimes find that it helps you to understand the job better. For that reason, I am not a purist about doing things in a specific order. You do what works best for you.

The WBS does not have to be symmetrical. That is, all paths need not be broken down to Level 6 (or whatever level you stop at). Since the rule is to break work down to a level sufficient to achieve the estimating accuracy you desire, one path may take six levels, while another may need only three.

> **The WBS does not have to be symmetrical. All paths do not have to go down to the same level.**

Uses of the WBS

As I have said, the WBS is a good way to show the scope of a job. If you have ever given someone an estimate for a project cost or time and have seen her horrified look, you know she is seeing the project in her mind as much simpler than it is. When you show a project in WBS form, it is clear to most individuals why the job costs so much. In fact, I have had the experience of finding the planning group members themselves overwhelmed by the complexity and magnitude of the WBS. If it impresses them, think of its impact on an outsider.

> **The WBS is a good way to portray the scope of a project.**

Assigning responsibility for tasks is another important use of the WBS. Each task to be performed should be assigned to a particular person who will be responsible for its completion. These assignments can then be listed on a separate form, often called a responsibility chart (see figure 7-4).

[FIGURE 7-4]
RESPONSIBILITY CHART

Linear Responsibility Chart														
Project:	Date Issued:			Sheet Number:			of							
Manager:	Date Revised:			Revision No.		File: LRCFORM.61								
	Project Contributors													
Task Descriptions														
CODES: 1 = ACTUAL RESPONSIBILITY; 2 = SUPPORT; 3 = MUST BE NOTIFIED; BLANK = NOT INVOLVED														

Estimating Time, Costs, and Resources

Once the work is broken down, you can estimate how long it will take. But how? Suppose I ask you how long it will take to sort a standard deck of playing cards that has been thoroughly shuffled into numerical order by suit. How would you answer that question?

The most obvious way would be to try the task several times and get a feeling for it. But if you didn't have a deck of cards handy, you would probably think about it, *imagine* how long it would take, and give me an answer. People generally give me answers ranging from two minutes to ten minutes. My tests indicate that about three minutes is average for most adults.

....

An estimate can be made only by starting with the assumption that a certain resource will be assigned.

....

Suppose, however, we gave the cards to a child about four or five years old. It might take a lot longer, since the child would not be that familiar with the sequence in which cards are ordered and perhaps might not yet be that comfortable with counting. So we must reach a very important conclusion: You cannot do a time or cost estimate without considering who will actually perform the task. Second, you must base the estimate on historical data or a mental model. Historical data are best.

Generally, we use average times to plan projects. That is, if it takes three minutes on average for adults to sort a deck of cards, I would use three minutes as my estimate of how long it will take during execution of my project. Naturally, when I use averages, in reality some tasks will take longer than the time allowed, and some should take less. Overall, however, they should *average out*.

That is the idea, anyway. Parkinson's Law discredits this notion, however. Parkinson said that work always expands to fill the time allowed. That means that tasks may take longer than the estimated time, but they almost never take less. One reason is that when people find themselves with some time left, they tend to refine what they have done. Another is that people fear that if they turn work in early, they may be expected to do the task faster the next time or that they may be given more work to do.

> **Parkinson's Law: Work expands to fill the time allowed.**

This is a very important point: if people are penalized for performing better than the target, they will quit doing so. We also have to understand *variation*. If the same person sorts a deck of cards over and over, we know the sort times will vary. Sometimes it will take two minutes, while other times it will take four. The average may be three, but we may expect that half the time it will take three minutes or less and half the time it will take three minutes or more. Very seldom will it take exactly three minutes.

> **We must be careful not to penalize workers who perform better than expected by loading them down with excessive work.**

The same is true for *all* project tasks. The time it takes to perform them will vary because of forces outside the person's control. The cards are shuffled differently every time. The person's attention is diverted by a loud noise outside. He drops a card while sorting. He gets tired. And so on.

Can you get rid of the variation? No way.

Can you reduce it? Yes—through practice, by changing the process by which the work is done, and so on. But it is important to note that the variation will always be there, and we must recognize and accept it.

The Hazards of Estimating

Consider the case of Karen. One day, her boss stopped by her desk at about one o'clock. "Need for you to do an estimate for me," he told her. "Promised the Big Guy I'd have it for him by four o'clock. You with me?"

Karen nodded and gave him a thin smile. The boss described the job for her. "Just need a ballpark number," he assured her and drifted off.

Given so little time, Karen could compare the project her boss described only to one she had done about a year before. She added a little for this and took a little off for that, put in some contingency to cover her lack of information, and gave the estimate to the boss. After that, she forgot all about the job.

Two months passed. Then the bomb was dropped. Her boss appeared, all smiles. "Remember that estimate you did for me on the XYZ job?"

She had to think hard to remember, but, as her boss droned on, it came back to her. He piled a big stack of specifications on her desk. "It's your job now," he told her and drifted off again into manager dreamland.

As she studied the pile of paper, Karen felt herself growing more concerned. There were significant differences between this set of specs and what her boss had told her when she did the estimate. "Oh well, I'm sure he knows that," she told herself.

Finally, she managed to work up a new estimate for the job on the basis of the real specs. It was almost 50 percent higher than the ballpark figure. She checked her figures carefully, assured herself that they were correct, and went to see her boss.

He took one look at the numbers and went ballistic. "What are you trying to do to me?" he yelled. "I already told the old man we would do it for the original figure. I can't tell him it's this much more. He'll kill me."

"But you told me it was just a ballpark number you needed," Karen argued. "That's what I gave you. This is nothing like the job I quoted. It's a lot bigger."

"I can't help that," her boss argued. "I already gave him the figures. You'll have to find a way to do it for the original bid."

> One of the primary causes of project failures is that ballpark estimates become targets.

Naturally, you know the rest of the story. The job cost even more than Karen's new estimate. There was a lot of moaning and groaning, but, in the end, Karen survived. Oh, they did send her off to a course on project management—hoping, no doubt, that she would learn how to estimate better in the future.

Suggestions for Effective Estimating

The American Management Association highlights several approaches for project managers to develop good, solid estimates.

Historical Data

Learn from the past. Historical data can be considered the best source for project estimates. How long did this task take to complete last time? How much did this subassembly cost? If the historical data have integrity—meaning that they have not been contaminated—use these data as you estimate project schedule / cost / resource requirements, and so on. Is it possible that the previous experiences were atypical? Yes. Do your research, but consider historical, actual data your best source for project estimates.

Level of Detail

Determine the required level of detail for your estimates. If you are in the early stages of project planning, high-level estimates should suffice. If you have completed your work breakdown structure and are deep into planning, you will typically take a more detailed approach. The smaller the unit of the work, the more accurate your estimate is likely to be.

Ownership of the Estimate

If the individual supplying the estimate *owns* it, it is likely to be more accurate. Consider the team member estimating the duration to complete a task, knowing that because her name will be associated with the estimate, she will be held accountable. The team member now owns the estimate and will invest more time and effort to produce a more accurate number. If no ownership exists, the team member may try to "wing it."

Human Productivity

Project managers, team members, and others supporting the project cannot be expected to be 100 percent productive during the course of a working day. This would not be realistic. People are distracted, call in sick, move in and out of the project, and so on.

In figure 7-5, you can see that the standard forty-hour, five-day week must be adjusted to take into account project loss (15 percent), reworks/debugs (10 percent), and labor overhead (15 percent). As the figure shows, the estimated total required hours is fifty-six, not forty, and the estimated required number of days is seven, not five.

[FIGURE 7-5]

HUMAN PRODUCTIVITY

Productivity Factor	Hours	Cost/Hour	Labor Cost	Duration
Base Estimate	40	$75	$3,000	5.00
Project Loss (15%)	6	$75	$450	0.75
Rework/Debug (10%)	4	$75	$300	0.50
Subtotal (Direct Cost)	50	$75	$3,750	6.25
Labor Overhead	6	-	-	0.75
Total For Scheduling	56	-	-	7.00

Project managers must work in the real world. We accomplish work within the triple constraints triangle of scope, time, and cost (see figure 11-1 on page 161). Consequently, the realities of human productivity must be considered whenever estimates are calculated.

Time/Cost/Resource Trade-Off

When estimating in the project environment, don't forget the human dynamic. Team members are not robots, yet.

Figure 7-6 demonstrates what typically results when an individual is working on multiple tasks. The stops and starts create inefficiencies. She must stop one task and ramp up to begin another, reducing productivity. Conversely, if a task will be shared by more than one individual, inefficiencies appear in the form of additional communication requirements, possible conflicts, and the need to identify logical break points between workers.

[FIGURE 7-6]

TIME, COST, RESOURCE TRADE-OFF

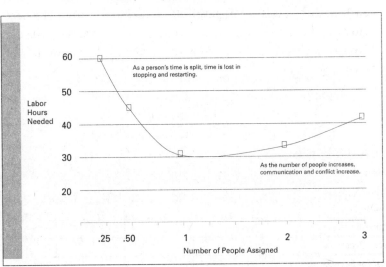

Distribution of Estimates

Distribution adds knowledge and common sense to the estimating process. Using only worst-case assumptions will generate arbitrarily high estimates. Using only best-case assumptions will likely set your project up for failure, as everything must go right to achieve the estimate. The most likely estimate should rely on experience and account for reality. It is here that the project manager takes the temperature of the project. She takes into account project constraints and variables and determines what should be considered most likely *today.*

Using these concepts, the project manager can apply simple formulas to improve estimation accuracy. The *three-point estimates* technique is used to identify the level of uncertainty in an estimate. Three sets of estimates are produced for a project activity using three different sets of assumptions. The first is the *optimistic,* or best-case, estimate; the second is the *pessimistic,* or worst-case, estimate; and the third is the *most likely* estimate. This allows you to calculate the *standard average.* As you can see in figure 7-7, you add the three points and then divide by three. The result is a number that considers all possibilities and gives you a working estimate.

> The *three-point estimates* technique is used to identify the level of uncertainty in an estimate using three sets of assumptions: the *optimistic* estimate, the *pessimistic* estimate, and the *most likely* estimate.

The Program Evaluation and Review Technique (PERT) is a variation on three-point estimating. It was developed in 1957 to support the Polaris missile submarine program by an operations research team staffed with representatives from the Operations Research Department of Booz Allen Hamilton; the Evaluation Office of the Lockheed Missile Systems Division; and the Program Evaluation Branch, Special Projects Office, of the Department of the Navy.

[FIGURE 7-7]

CALCULATING THE STANDARD AVERAGE

Improving Accuracy Using Three-Point Estimates

$$\text{Standard average} = \frac{O + ML + P}{3}$$

Key: O = Optimistic estimate | ML = Most likely estimate | P = Pessimistic estimate

Many projects are unique efforts that include tasks that have not been done before. Consequently, no historical data are available. PERT has proved a very useful tool when estimating in this type of project environment. It works especially well when there is this high degree of uncertainty, as the pessimistic estimate can be extremely high. This approach also allows the project manager to apply weight to the most likely estimate based on experience and the current situation. The difference between it and the standard average approach is that PERT contains a *weighting factor*, so it is a weighted average. You are adding weight to the most likely estimate (ML) because, based on experience and the current situation, you think that will be the most probable outcome. The most likely estimate in figure 7-8 is weighted by a factor of 4 (4ML). ML is counted four times, and optimistic and pessimistic estimates one time each, yielding a total of six values. This is why you divide by six when determining the PERT weighted average.

The *PERT* technique of estimating is a variation on three-point estimating that contains a weighting factor.

[FIGURE 7-8]

CALCULATING THE PERT WEIGHTED AVERAGE

Improving Accuracy Using Three-Point Estimates

$$(\text{PERT}) \text{ weighted average} = \frac{O + 4ML + P}{6}$$

Key: O = Optimistic estimate | ML = Most likely estimate | P = Pessimistic estimate

Many project managers think that the final estimate will always be close to the most likely value (ML) because of the weighting factor. While that is often true and appropriate, the uncertainty of the project environment often drives the pessimistic value higher, resulting in a better overall estimate.

Remember, estimates are predictions. They are projections into the future that are inherently uncertain. Use your subject matter experts! Nobody knows the work and can estimate more accurately than they can. As your project matures and you become smarter, you can adjust and update your estimates.

Improving Estimating Ability

People cannot learn unless they receive feedback on their performance. If you went out every day and ran one hundred yards, trying to improve your speed but never timing yourself, you would have no idea whether you were getting better or worse. You could be doing something that slowed you down, but you wouldn't know it. In the same way, if you estimate task durations but never record the actual time it takes to do the task, you are never going to get better at estimating. Furthermore, you have to track progress by recording times daily. If you record times once a week, I can promise you that you will be just guessing, and that won't be helpful.

Project Procurement Management

As the WBS portrays the scope of project work, it also provides necessary insight regarding the nature of tasks and activities. Many project managers discover that some of the work requires the procurement of goods and/or services from an outside source. This is not cause for panic, but if you have not used purchase orders or contracts on previous projects, you should know some basics as you enter the world of procurement.

Think about anything you have bought in your personal life that required delivery. Is everything delivered on time? Did you receive exactly what you ordered or expected? As a graduate of the Northrop Grumman procurement and project worlds, I assure you that not every procured item will be on time and acceptable. All project managers must plan and manage procured goods and services to ensure a smooth procurement process.

When procuring goods and services from suppliers and vendors, project managers must ask three questions:

- What must be procured?
- When is it needed?
- How will it be acquired?

The project manager (or a team member) will then take the next step and request cost and pricing data. Depending on your industry and other factors, this can be as simple as an email or considerably more complex. It could even include various clauses and terms and conditions.

Review previous projects, interview colleagues with buying experience, and check your regulations! At Northrop Grumman, I was bound by the Federal Acquisition Regulations (FAR), with its significant number of rules and requirements. Commercial purchasing is far less regulated and allows you much more freedom. If you are not sure . . . ask.

General request guidelines include the following:

- *Request for Information (RFI)*. This is usually a simple request to potential sellers asking for information regarding the product/services they sell. There is no implied commitment to buy from them.
- *Request for Quote (RFQ)*. This is most often used for standard or off-the-shelf goods or services.
- *Request for Proposal (RFP)*. This asks potential suppliers to propose how their goods or services can achieve a specific outcome, along with pricing.
- Sellers and buyers will often use RFQ and RFP to refer to the same process. This is not a cause for concern; it likely reflects a personal preference.
- Once the seller is chosen, a purchase order (PO) or contract is the next logical step. Common PO types for project managers include:
  - *Firm Fixed Price*. The price is agreed upon up front and is not subject to adjustment or change.
  - *Cost Plus Reimbursement*. The buyer pays the seller's costs plus an agreed-upon profit.
  - *Time and Materials*. The buyer pays for the seller's time plus any materials the seller was required to purchase.

I was introduced to *best value procurement* while working for Grumman Aerospace, where I had to adhere to the Federal Acquisition Regulations. There was an effort within the Department of Defense to add more rigor to the purchasing process. The goal was to determine who were the best overall suppliers and vendors, not just the cheapest. You can add that same rigor to your project purchases.

Don't always circle the low bidder! Sometimes the lowest bidder will not prove to be the best choice for the project. Does this seller have a history with you, your colleagues, or your organization? Find out. Do your research, make some phone calls, send some emails. If you learn that the seller is often or always late, and this procurement is schedule sensitive, the low bidder may cost you project success. If you are purchasing material and there is a history of rejections, analyze the possible impact these rejections might have on your schedule and budget. Strive to choose the seller that provides you with the best overall value, including quality, on-time performance, accessibility, and price. Best value procurement helps you avoid the lowest bid becoming the highest cost to the project.

If you have a procurement department, use it. Always leverage your institutional expertise. Project managers will occasionally try to "go it alone" because they fear getting slowed down or involving too many people. This is a bad idea. I nearly *always* sought out my procurement contacts because they had the answers. At the very least, I knew they would steer me clear of the bad suppliers, the historically poor performers. They may also recommend the *winners*, those who have performed very well in the past.

The last project I managed at Northrop Grumman involved the creation of an organization-wide supplier performance rating system. Many procurement departments have this system in place and can provide you with comprehensive data regarding the performance of suppliers that you need to buy from. Talk to your procurement people, and use those data if they exist. They may even have a preferred supplier list for you to review.

As you plan your project, it may become apparent that purchased parts or services will affect a significant portion of your budget and/or schedule. When this is the case, try to recruit a full- or part-time team member who will represent the procurement department. If you don't have a procurement department, reach out to a purchasing agent or an experienced buyer. It is always good to include an SME to help you steer the course.

KEY POINTS TO REMEMBER

- Do not try to work out sequencing of activities when you develop a WBS. You will do that when you develop a schedule.
- A WBS ties the entire project together. It portrays scope graphically, allows you to assign resources, permits you to develop estimates of time and costs, and thus provides the basis for the schedule and the budget.
- An estimate is a *guess*, and an exact estimate is an *oxymoron*!
- Be careful that ballpark estimates don't become targets.
- The *three-point estimates* technique is used to identify the level of uncertainty in an estimate.
- PERT is an excellent approach to estimating when uncertainty is high.
- Use your procurement department. If you do not have one, check with a purchasing agent or do your research.
- No learning takes place without feedback. Estimate, then track your actual time if you want to improve your estimating ability.

EXERCISE

Following is a list of tasks to be performed in preparation for a camping trip. Draw a WBS that places the tasks in their proper relationship to one another. The solution can be found in the Answers section.

- Arrange for supplies and equipment.
- Select campsite.
- Make site preparations.
- Make site reservation.
- Arrange time off from work.
- Select route to site.
- Prepare menu for meals.
- Identify source of supplies and equipment.
- Load car.
- Pack suitcases.
- Purchase supplies.
- Arrange camping trip (project).

CHAPTER 8

SCHEDULING PROJECT WORK

One of the primary features that distinguishes project management from general management is the special attention to scheduling. Remember from chapter 1 that Dr. J. M. Juran says a project is a problem scheduled for solution.

Project management is not *just* scheduling.

Unfortunately, some people think that project management is nothing but scheduling, and this is incorrect. Scheduling is just one of the tools used to manage jobs and should not be considered the primary one.

People today tend to acquire scheduling software, of which there is an abundance, and think that will make them instant project managers. They soon find that that idea is wrong. In fact, it is nearly impossible to use the software effectively unless you understand project management (and scheduling methodology in particular).

....

Suggestion: Whatever scheduling software you choose, get some professional training on how to use it.

....

I do have one suggestion about software. Whatever you pick, get some professional training on how to use it. In the early days of personal computers, there was a pretty significant difference between low-end and high-end software that was available. The low-end packages were pretty easy to use, whereas the high-end ones were not. The gap between low- and high-end software has closed to the point that this is no longer true. They are all difficult to use now, and the training materials (tutorials and manuals) that come with the software are often not very good. In addition, it is hard to find time to work through a tutorial without being interrupted several times, which means that self-learning is difficult. The most efficient way is to take a class.

Do check out the instructor's knowledge of project management before choosing which class to take. Some of the people teaching the software know very little about project management itself, and, when you have questions, they can't answer them.

You should expect to spend from two to three days of classroom time becoming really proficient with the software. That is still a good investment, considering the time the software can save you in the long run.

A Brief History of Scheduling

Until around 1958, the only tool for scheduling projects was the bar chart (see figure 8-1). Because Henry Gantt developed a complete notational system for showing progress with bar charts, they are often called Gantt charts. They are simple to construct and read and remain the best tool to use for communicating to team members what they need to do within given time frames. Arrow diagrams tend to be too complicated for some teams. Nevertheless, it is often helpful to show an arrow diagram to the people doing the work so that they understand interdependencies and why it is important that they complete certain tasks on time.

[FIGURE 8-1]

BAR CHART

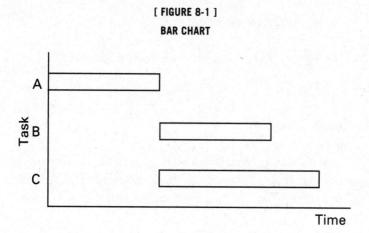

Bar charts do have one serious drawback: it is very difficult to determine the impact of a slip on one task on the rest of the project (e.g., if Task A in figure 8-1 gets behind, it is hard to tell how this will affect the rest of the work). The reason is that the bar chart (in its original format) did not show the interdependencies of the work. (Contemporary software does show links between bars, making them easier to read. The actual name for this bar chart is *time-line critical path schedule*.)

To overcome this problem, two methods of scheduling were developed in the late 1950s and early 1960s, both of which use arrow diagrams to capture the sequential and parallel relationships among project activities. One of these methods, developed by DuPont, is called the *Critical Path Method* (CPM), and the other is the previously discussed *Program Evaluation and Review Technique* (PERT, see chapter 7). Although it has become customary to call all arrow diagrams PERT networks, strictly speaking the PERT method makes use of probability techniques, whereas CPM does not. In other words, with PERT it is possible to calculate the probability that an activity will be completed by a certain time, whereas that is not possible with CPM.

....

CPM: Critical Path Method

PERT: Program Evaluation and Review Technique

....

Network Diagrams

To show the sequence in which work is performed, diagrams like those in figure 8-2 are used. In these diagrams, Task A is done before B, while Task C is done in parallel with them.

[FIGURE 8-2]
ARROW DIAGRAMS

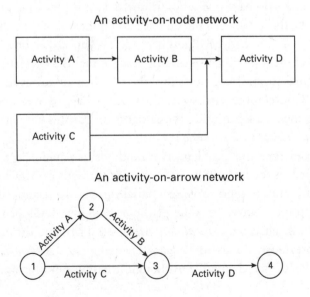

An activity-on-node network

An activity-on-arrow network

The network in the bottom half of figure 8-2 uses *activity-on-arrow* notation, in which the arrows represent the work being done, and the circles represent events. An event is *binary*; that is, it has either occurred or it has not. An activity, on the other hand, can be partially complete. Note that this is a special use of the word "event." We speak of a football game as an event, even though it spans time. In scheduling terminology, however, an *event* is a specific point in time where something has just started or has just been finished.

The network in the top half of figure 8-2 uses *activity-on-node* notation, which shows the work as a box or node, and the arrows show the sequence in which the work is performed. Events are not shown in activity-on-node networks unless they are *milestones*—points in the project at which major portions of the work are completed.

Why two forms of diagrams? Probably a tyranny to confuse the uninitiated. Actually, it simply happens that the schemes were developed by different practitioners.

Is one better than the other? No. They both get the same results in figuring out when work is supposed to be completed. Both forms are still used, although activity-on-node is used a bit more than the other, simply because much of today's personal computer software is programmed to use node notation.

> The *critical path* is the longest path through a project network. Because it has no slack, all activities on the critical path must be completed as scheduled, or the end date will begin to slip—one day for each day a critical activity is delayed.

What is the benefit of using either CPM or PERT? The main advantage is that you can tell whether it is possible to meet an important project completion date, and you can also tell exactly when various tasks must be finished in order to meet that deadline.

Furthermore, you can tell which tasks have some leeway and which do not. In fact, both CPM and PERT determine the *critical path*, which is defined as the longest series of activities (that can't be done in parallel) and which therefore governs how early the project can be completed.

The Reason for Scheduling

Naturally, the primary reason for scheduling a project is to ensure that the deadline can be met. Most projects have a deadline imposed. Furthermore, since the critical path method helps identify which activities will determine the end date, it also helps guide how the project should be managed.

However, it is easy to get carried away with scheduling and spend all of your time updating, revising, and so on. The scheduling software in use today should be viewed as a *tool*, and managers should not become slaves to the tool.

It is also very easy to create schedules that look good on paper but don't work in practice. The main reason is usually that resources are not available to do the work when it comes due. In fact, unless resource allocation is handled properly, schedules are next to useless. Fortunately, today's scheduling software handles resource allocation fairly well, but we leave discussion of the methods used to the software manuals. In this book, we simply examine how networks are used to show us where we need to manage.

I am often told that scope and priorities change so often in a given organization that it doesn't make sense to spend time finding critical paths. Two points are worth considering here. One is that if scope is changing often in a project, not enough time is being spent doing up-front definition and planning. Scope changes most often occur because something is forgotten. Better attention to what is being done in the beginning usually reduces scope creep.

Second, if priorities are changing often, management does not have its act together. Generally, the organization is trying to tackle too much work for the resources available. We all have wish lists of things we want to do personally, but we have to put some of them on hold until time, money, or both become available. The same is true of organizations. Experience shows that when you have individuals working on many projects, productivity suffers. One company found, as an example, that when it stopped having people work on multiple projects, employees' productivity *doubled*! That obviously is highly significant.

> **One company found that when it stopped having people work on multiple projects, workers' productivity *doubled*.**

What does CPM have to do with this? Knowing where the critical path is in a project allows you to determine the impact on the project of a scope or priority change. You know which activities will be impacted most heavily and what might need to be done to regain lost time. In addition, managers can make informed decisions when you can tell them the impact of changes to the project. Thus, CPM can be an invaluable tool when used properly.

DEFINITIONS OF NETWORK TERMS

ACTIVITY: An *activity* always consumes time and may also consume resources. Examples include paperwork, labor negotiations, machinery operations, and lead times for purchased parts or equipment.

CRITICAL ACTIVITY: A *critical activity* or event is one that must be achieved by a certain time, having no latitude (slack or float) whatsoever.

CRITICAL PATH: The *critical path* is the longest path through a network and determines the earliest completion of project work.

EVENTS: Beginning and ending points of activities are known as
events. An *event* is a specific point in time. Events are commonly denoted graphically by a circle and may carry identity
nomenclature (e.g., words, numbers, alphanumeric codes).

MILESTONE: A *milestone* is an event that represents a point in a
project of special significance. Usually, it is the completion of
a major phase of the work. Project reviews are often conducted at milestones.

NETWORK: *Networks* are called arrow diagrams. They provide a
graphical representation of a project plan showing the relationships of the activities.

Constructing an Arrow Diagram

As was pointed out in chapter 7, a work breakdown structure
(WBS) should be developed before work on the project is scheduled. Also, we saw that a WBS can contain from two to twenty
levels. To illustrate how a schedule is constructed from a WBS, we
consider a simple job of maintaining the yard around a home. The
WBS is shown in figure 8-3.

In the case of this WBS, it is appropriate to schedule the tasks
at the lowest level. However, this is not always true. Sometimes
work is broken down to Level 6, but only activities up to Level 5
are entered into the schedule. The reason is that you may not be
able to keep Level 6 tasks on schedule. That is, you can't manage
that tightly. So you schedule at a level that you can manage. This
follows the general rule that you should never plan (or schedule)
in more detail than you *can* manage. Some projects, such as over-
hauling a large power generator, are scheduled in increments of
hours. Others are scheduled in days, while some big construction
jobs are scheduled to the nearest month.

While planning in too much detail is undesirable, if you plan
in too little detail, you might as well not bother. As a practical

[FIGURE 8-3]

WBS TO DO YARD PROJECT

example, a manager told me that his staff wanted to create schedules showing tasks with twenty-six-week durations. He protested that the staff would never complete such schedules on time. They would *back-end-load* them, he argued.

What he meant was that there is a lot of security in a twenty-six-week task. When the start date comes, if the person doing the task is busy, she might say, "I can always make up a day on a twenty-six-week activity. I'll get started tomorrow." This continues until she realizes she has delayed too long. Then there is a big flurry of activity as she tries to finish on time. All the work has been pushed out to the end of the twenty-six-week time frame.

A good rule of thumb to follow is that no task should have a duration much greater than four to six weeks. A twenty-six-week task can probably be broken down into five or six subtasks. Such a plan generally keeps people from back-end loading.

There are two ways you can develop a schedule. One is to begin at the end and work back until you arrive at the beginning. The second method is to start at the beginning and work toward the end. Usually, it is easiest to start at the beginning.

The first step is to decide what can be done first. Sometimes, several tasks can start at the same time. In that case, you simply draw them side by side and start working from there. Note the progression in the diagram in figure 8-4. It sometimes takes several iterations before the sequencing can be worked out completely.

[FIGURE 8-4]

CPM DIAGRAM FOR YARD PROJECT

This small project might be thought of as having three phases: *preparation, execution,* and *cleanup.* There are three preparation tasks: *pick up trash, put gas in equipment,* and *get out hedge clipper.* The cleanup tasks include *bagging grass, bundling clippings,* and *hauling trash to the dump.*

In doing this schedule diagram, I have followed a rule of scheduling, which is to *diagram what is logically possible, then deal with resource limitations.* For a yard project, if I have no one helping me, then there really can be no parallel paths. On the other hand, if I can enlist help from the family or neighborhood youth, then parallel paths are possible, so this rule says go ahead and schedule as *if* it were possible to get help. This is especially important to remember in a work setting, or you will never get a schedule put together. You will be worrying about who will be available to do the work and end up in analysis paralysis.

> **Schedules should be developed according to what is logically possible, and resource allocation should be done later. This will yield the *optimum* schedule.**

Another rule is to keep all times in the same increments. Don't mix hours and minutes—schedule everything in minutes, then convert to hours and minutes as a last step. For this schedule, I have simply kept everything in minutes.

> **Another rule is to keep all times in the same increments.**

I suggest that you draw your network on paper and check it for logical consistency before entering anything into a computer scheduling program. If the network has logical errors, the computer will just give you a *garbage-in/garbage-out* result, but it will look impressive, having come from a computer.

> **It is hard to tell whether a network is absolutely correct, but it can be said to be wrong if logic is violated.**

It is also important to remember that there is usually no *single* solution to a network problem. That is, someone else might draw the arrow diagram a bit differently than you have done. There may be parts of the diagram that *have* to be done in a certain order, but often there is flexibility. For example, you can't deliver papers until you have printed them, so if the diagram showed that sequence, it would be wrong. The conclusion is that there is no single right solution, but a diagram can be said to be wrong if it violates logic.

The network for the yard project could get a lot more complicated. You could have *edge front sidewalk* and *edge back sidewalk*. You could talk about trimming around trees in both front and back, and so on. But there is no need to make it so complicated. We don't usually try to capture *exactly* how we will do the work, just the gist of it.

The next step is to figure out how long it will take to do the job. Time estimates for each task are made by using history, taking into account how long each activity has taken in the past. Remember, though, that the estimate is valid only for the individual who is going to do the task. If my daughter, who is sixteen, does the lawn mowing using a push mower, it will probably take less time than if my son, who is only twelve, does the same task. In the following chapter, we see how to find the critical path through the network so that we can know how long things will take.

KEY POINTS TO REMEMBER

- ♦ Project management is not just scheduling.
- ♦ Arrow diagrams allow an easier assessment of the impact of a slip on a project than is possible with Gantt charts.
- ♦ Schedule at a level of detail that can be managed.
- ♦ No task should be scheduled with a duration much greater than four to six weeks. Subdivide longer tasks to achieve this objective.

EXERCISE

For the following WBS (figure 8-5), draw an arrow diagram. One solution is shown in the Answers section.

[FIGURE 8-5]

WBS TO CLEAN ROOM

CHAPTER 9

PRODUCING A WORKABLE SCHEDULE

O nce a suitable network has been drawn, with durations assigned to all activities, it is necessary to determine where the longest path is in the network and to see whether it will meet the target completion date. Since the longest path through the project determines *minimum* project duration, any activity on that path that takes longer than planned will cause the end date to slip accordingly, so that path is called the *critical path*.

Schedule Computations

Normally, you would let a computer do these computations for you, so you may wonder why it is necessary to know how to do them manually. My belief is that unless you know how the computations are done, you do not fully understand the meanings of float, early and late dates, and so on. Further, you can easily fall prey to the garbage-in/garbage-out malady. So here is a brief treatment of how the calculations are done by the computer. (For most schedules, the computer has the added bonus of converting times to calendar dates, which is no easy task to do manually.)

First, consider what we want to know about the project. If it starts at some *time = 0*, we want to know how soon it can be finished. Naturally, in most actual work projects, we have been told when we must be finished. That is, the end date is dictated. Furthermore, the start date for the job is often constrained for some reason: resources won't be available, specs won't be written, or another project won't be finished until that time. So scheduling usually means trying to fit the work between two fixed points in time. Whatever the case, we still want to know how long the project will take to complete; if it won't fit into the required time frame, then we will have to do something to shorten the critical path.

In the simplest form, network computations are made for the network on the assumption that activity durations are exactly as specified. However, activity durations are a function of the level of resources applied to the work, and, if that level is not actually available when it comes time to do the work, then the scheduled dates for the task cannot be met.

> **Failure to consider resource allocation in scheduling almost always leads to a schedule that cannot be achieved.**

It is for this reason that network computations must ultimately be made with resource limitations in mind. Another way to say this is that *resource allocation* is necessary to determine what kind of schedule is actually *achievable*! Failure to consider resources almost always leads to a schedule that cannot be met.

> **Initial schedule computations are made assuming that unlimited resources are available. This yields the *best-case solution*.**

Still, the first step in network computations is to determine where the critical path is in the schedule and what kind of latitude is available for noncritical work, under *ideal conditions*. Naturally, the ideal situation is one in which unlimited resources are available, so the first computations made for the network are done without consideration of resource requirements. It is this method that is described in this chapter, and resource allocation methods are deferred to scheduling software manuals, as previously stated.

Network Rules

To compute network start and finish times, only two rules apply to all networks. See the following Rules 1 and 2. Other rules are sometimes applied by the scheduling software itself. These are strictly a function of the software and are not applied to all networks.

RULE 1: Before a task can begin, all tasks preceding it must be completed.

RULE 2: Arrows denote the logical order of work.

Basic Scheduling Computations

Scheduling computations are illustrated using the network in figure 9-1. First, let us examine the node boxes in the schedule. Each has the notation ES, LS, EF, LF, or DU:

ES = Early Start
LS = Late Start
EF = Early Finish
LF = Late Finish
DU = Duration (of the task)

Forward-Pass Computations

Consider a single activity in the network, such as picking up trash from the yard. It has a duration of fifteen minutes. Assuming that it starts at time = 0, it can finish as early as fifteen minutes later. Thus, we can enter 15 in the cell labeled "EF."

[FIGURE 9-1]

NETWORK TO ILLUSTRATE COMPUTATION METHODS

Putting gas in the mower and the weed whacker takes only five minutes. The logic of the diagram says that both of these tasks must be completed before we can begin trimming weeds, cutting the front grass, and edging the sidewalk. The cleanup task takes fifteen minutes, whereas the gas activity takes only five minutes. How soon can the following activities start? Not until the cleanup has been finished, since it is the longest of the preceding activities.

In fact, then, the Early Finish for cleanup becomes the Early Start for the next three tasks. It is always true that the latest Early Finish for preceding tasks becomes the Early Start for subsequent tasks. That is, the longest path determines how early subsequent tasks can start.

....

The Earliest Start for a task is the *latest* Late Finish of preceding tasks. That is, the longest path determines the earliest that a following task can be started.

....

Following this rule, we can fill in Earliest Start times for each task, as shown in figure 9-2. This shows that the project will take a total of 165 minutes to complete, if all work is conducted exactly as shown. We have just performed what are called *forward-pass computations* to determine Earliest Finish times for all activities. Computer programs do exactly the same thing and additionally convert the times to calendar dates, making quick work of the computations.

[FIGURE 9-2]
DIAGRAM WITH EF TIMES FILLED IN

RULE: When two or more activities precede another activity, the earliest time when that activity can be started is the *longer* of the durations of the activities preceding it.

NOTE: The time determined for the end or final event is the earliest finish for the project in working time. Once weekends, holidays, and other breaks in the schedule are accounted for, the end *date* may be considerably later than the earliest finish in working time.

Backward-Pass Computations

A *backward pass* is made through the network to compute the *latest start* and *latest finish times* for each activity in the network. To do that, we must decide how late the project can finish. By convention, we generally don't want a project to end any later than its earliest possible completion. To stretch it out longer would be inefficient.

We also won't insist (for now) that the project end earlier than the earliest possible finish calculated in the previous steps. If we want to finish earlier, we will have to redraw the network or shorten some activities (e.g., by applying more resources or working more efficiently). For now, we will accept the 165-minute working time and let it be the *Latest Finish* for the project.

If Hauling Away Trash has a Late Finish of 165 minutes and a duration of 45 minutes, what is the latest that it could start? Clearly, if we subtract 45 from 165, we have 120 minutes, which is the Latest Start for the task. Proceeding in this manner, we get LS times for Bagging Grass and Bundling Clippings of 90 and 105 minutes, respectively. One of these two numbers must be the LF time for each of the preceding activities. Which one?

Well, assume we try 105 minutes. If we do that, the schedule would say that Bagging Grass could start as late as 105 minutes, since subsequent tasks can begin as soon as preceding tasks are finished. But if we add 30 minutes for Bagging to the 105-minute ES time, we will finish at 135 minutes, which is later than the 120 minutes previously determined, and we will miss the 165-minute end time for the project.

Therefore, when we are doing *backward-pass calculations*, the *Latest Finish* for a preceding task will always be the *smallest* of the

Late Start times for the subsequent tasks. (A simpler way to say this is: always use the smallest number!)

> **When doing backward-pass calculations, always use the smallest number for the Latest Finish of previous activities.**

RULE: When two or more activities follow another, the latest time that the preceding activity can be achieved is the *smaller* of the times.

Now examine the path in figure 9-3, which includes activities highlighted by bold lines. Each activity has the same ES/LS and EF/LF times. There is no *float* (or latitude for slippage) on this path. By convention, an activity with no float is called *critical*, and a total path with no float is called the *critical path*, which means that if any of the work on this path falls behind schedule, then the end date will slip accordingly. All of the activities that have ES/LS or EF/LF times that differ are said to have float. For example, Trim Weeds has an ES time of fifteen minutes and an LS time of sixty minutes, giving it forty-five minutes of float.

> **When an activity has no float, it is called *critical*, since failure to complete the work as scheduled will cause the end date to slip.**

The final network is shown in figure 9-3. Note that some tasks have the same EF and LF times, as well as the same ES and LS times. These tasks are on the *critical path*. In figure 9-3, they are shown with bold outlines, to indicate exactly where the critical path lies.

The critical path activities have no latitude. They must be completed as scheduled, or the entire project will take longer than 165

[FIGURE 9-3]

DIAGRAM SHOWING CRITICAL PATH

minutes. Knowing where the critical path is tells a manager where his attention must be applied. The other tasks have latitude, or float. This does not mean that they can be ignored, but they have less chance of delaying the project if they encounter problems. The Edge Sidewalk task, for example, has an ES time of fifteen minutes and an LS time of seventy-five. The difference between the two is sixty minutes, which is the float for the task.

What good is the float? Well, we know we can start the task as late as seventy-five minutes into the job and still finish the project on time. If your son is doing this task, he can watch a sixty-minute television program during that time and still get his Edging task done on time.

Remember, too, that the times are all *estimates*. This means that tasks might take more or less than the scheduled time. As long as they do not take longer than the scheduled time plus the available float time, the job can be completed on time. Critical tasks, which have no float, must be managed in such a way that they take the scheduled time. This is usually done by adjusting the resources (effort) applied, either by assigning more resources or by working overtime (increasing resources in either case).

This is not always possible. Applying overtime often increases errors, leading to rework, which may mean that you don't get the job done any faster than if you had just worked a normal schedule. Furthermore, there is always a point of diminishing returns when you add bodies to a task. At some point, they just get in each other's way, actually slowing work down rather than speeding it up. Note that overtime should be kept in reserve in case of problems, so it is never a good idea to schedule a project in a way that requires overtime just to meet the original schedule.

> It is bad practice to schedule a project so that overtime is required to meet the schedule, since if problems are encountered, it may not be possible to work more overtime to solve them.

Another point of great importance: all members of the project team should be encouraged to keep float times in reserve as insurance against bad estimates or unforeseen problems. People tend to wait until the latest possible start time to start a task; then, when problems occur, they miss the end date. If there is no float left, when the task takes longer than originally planned, it will impact the end date for the entire project, since, once a task runs out of float, it becomes part of the critical path! In fact, the true meaning of the word "critical" is that there is no float. The task must be done on time.

> Once you have used up the float on a task, it becomes part of the critical path.

Using the Network to Manage the Project

As I have indicated previously, the point of developing a CPM diagram is to use it to *manage* the project. If this is not done, scheduling is simply a worthless exercise. So here are some pointers that I have found helpful in managing my own jobs:

- Try to *stay on schedule*. It is always harder to catch up than to stay on target to begin with.
- Keep float in reserve in case of unexpected problems or bad estimates.
- Apply whatever effort is needed to keep critical tasks on schedule. If a task on the critical path can be finished ahead of schedule, *do it*! Then start the next task.
- Avoid the temptation to perfect everything—that's what the next-generation product or service is all about. Note: I *did not say* it is okay to do the job sloppily or that you shouldn't do your best work. I said don't be tempted to make it *perfect*. By definition, you will never reach perfection.
- Estimates of task durations are made on the assumption that certain people will work on those tasks. If someone else is actually used, you may have to adjust durations accordingly. This is especially true if the new person is less skilled than the intended resource.
- This was stated in chapter 8 but is repeated here because of its importance: no task should be scheduled with a duration much greater than four to six weeks. If you do, people tend to have a false sense of security and put off starting, under the assumption, "I can always make up one day." By the time they start, they often have slipped several days and find that they cannot finish as scheduled. We say that they *back-end-load* the task by pushing all the effort toward the back end. If a task has a duration greater than six weeks, it is a good idea to subdivide it, creating an artificial break if necessary. Then review progress at that point. That will help keep it on target.

- If the people doing the work did not develop the network, explain it to them and show them the meaning of float. Don't hide it from them. However, give them a bar chart to work with; it is much easier to read a bar chart than a network diagram. Show them that if they use up float on a given task, then the following tasks may become critical, leaving the people who must do those activities feeling really stressed.

- It is possible to shorten a task by adding resources, reducing its scope, doing sloppy (poor-quality) work, being more efficient, or changing the process by which the work is done. With the exception of doing sloppy work, all of the methods may be acceptable. A reduction in scope must be negotiated with your customer, of course.

- Scheduling is done initially on the assumption that you will have the resources you planned on having. If people are shared with other projects or if you plan to use the same person on several tasks, you may find that you have him overloaded. Modern software generally warns you that you have overloaded your resources and may be able to help you solve the problem.

Converting Arrow Diagrams to Bar Charts

While an arrow diagram is essential to do a proper analysis of the relationships between the activities in a project, the best working tool is the bar chart. The people doing the work will find it much easier to see when they are supposed to start and finish their jobs if you give them a bar chart. The arrow diagram in figure 9-3 has been portrayed as a bar chart in figure 9-4, making use of what was learned about the schedule from the network analysis.

Note that the critical path in the bar chart is shown as solid black bars. Bars with float are drawn hollow with a line trailing to indicate how much float is available. The task can end as late as the point at which the trailing line ends.

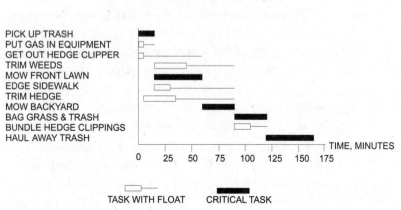

[FIGURE 9-4]

BAR CHART SCHEDULE FOR YARD PROJECT

This is fairly conventional notation. Scheduling software always allows you to print a bar chart, even though a CPM network is used to find the critical path and to calculate floats. One caution: Many programs display the critical path in red on a color monitor and the tasks that have been started with green or blue. When these bars are printed on a black-and-white printer, all of them may look black, implying that they are all critical, confusing the people trying to read them. It is usually possible to have the computer display shading or cross-hatching instead of color so that when they are printed in black-and-white, there is no ambiguity.

Assigning Resources to Tasks

I have already said that the first step in developing a schedule is to assume that you have unlimited resources because this is the best situation you can ever assume, and if you can't meet your project completion date with an unlimited resource schedule, you may as well know it early. However, once you have determined that the end date can somehow be met, you now must see whether your assumption of unlimited resources has overloaded your available resources.

Normally, you will find that you have people double- and triple-scheduled, which clearly won't work. These kinds of resource over-loads can be resolved only by using computer software, except for very simple schedules. This is where the software really excels, and yet estimates are that only a few percent of all the people who purchase software actually use it to level resources.

Consider the small schedule in figure 9-5. It contains only four tasks. Two are critical, and two have float. Task A requires two workers if it is to be completed in three weeks, and Tasks B and C need one person each. When it comes time to do the project, however, you find that only three workers are available. How did this happen?

[FIGURE 9-5]

SCHEDULE WITH RESOURCES OVERLOADED

It is possible that no more than three people were ever available, but because you followed the rule to schedule in parallel tasks that could logically be done in parallel, you inevitably overloaded your people. It is also possible that, when the plan was constructed, four workers were available but that one has since been assigned to another job that has priority over yours.

Whatever the reason, this schedule won't work unless something is changed. There are a number of possibilities and three areas to examine. You should first see whether any task has enough float to allow it to be delayed until resources become available. In this particular example, it turns out that this is possible. The solution is shown in figure 9-6.

[FIGURE 9-6]
SCHEDULE USING FLOAT TO LEVEL RESOURCES

Of course, this solution is a nice textbook example that just happens to work. It is never so easy in a real project. Notice that Task C has enough float that it can slide over and wait until Activity B is finished. But what usually happens is that Task C runs out of float before B is completed. Also, assume that Task D needs three people rather than two. As you can see, this complicates the situation considerably. This is shown in figure 9-7.

Since this is the typical situation, we must be prepared to handle it. There are two more places to look for help. The first is the functional relationship among the variables:

$$C = fx (P, T, S)$$

You should ask whether you can reduce scope, change the time limit, or reduce performance. Usually, performance is not

[FIGURE 9-7]
SCHEDULE WITH INADEQUATE FLOAT ON C TO PERMIT LEVELING

Time, weeks

negotiable, but the others may be. For example, sometimes you can reduce scope, and the project deliverable will still be acceptable to the client. Of course, if you can get another person for a short time, you won't have to consider reducing scope or performance. So you go shopping.

You ask the manager who "owns" the resources whether she can provide another person. She says sadly that she cannot and that she was even considering trying to take back another of the three she has already given you. Somehow you convince her not to do this. You then ask the project sponsor if it is okay to reduce scope. It is not.

It is also not okay to reduce performance. Nor can you find a contract employee in time to do the job. You are between a rock and a hard place. So you now ask whether there is another process that could be used to do the work. For example, if you can spray-paint a wall instead of using a roller, the task may go much faster.

Suppose you try this and again you come up empty-handed. You decide the only thing left to do is to resign your job. You never really wanted to be a project manager, anyway. But wait. Perhaps you can do something else.

Think back to what I said earlier. You use up all the float on C, and it is now a critical-path task. When you tell your software to level resources, it wants to know whether you want to schedule within the available float (or slack, as it is also called). If you say yes, as soon as a task runs out of float, it won't move over any further. This is also called *time-critical resource leveling* because time is of the essence for your project. (It always is!)

However, suppose you answer no to the question, "Do you want to level within the available slack?" In this case, you are telling the software to continue sliding tasks over until resources become available, even if it means slipping the end date. (This is called *resource-critical leveling*.) When you try this with our example schedule, you arrive at the solution shown in figure 9-8. Not bad, unless you can't live with the slip.

[FIGURE 9-8]

SCHEDULE UNDER RESOURCE-CRITICAL CONDITIONS

Time, weeks

In fact, sometimes the slip is so bad that it seems almost ridiculous. Your project was originally going to end in December of the current year. Now the software says it is so starved for resources that it will end in the year 2025! Ridiculous! What good is a schedule that goes out that far?

It can be used to bring the issue to everyone's attention. It shows the impact of inadequate resources and forces a trade-off, as described earlier—that is, if everyone believes your schedule in the first place. I had an experience with a fellow who said that he didn't believe the schedules in the first place because he thought they were always unrealistic, so an unrealistic schedule subjected to fancy calculations didn't prove anything to him.

I'm sure that's true. However, if people are willing to accept the limitations of what we are doing when we plan a project, this is at least a way of showing the limitations you face. Everyone must understand that estimating is *guessing*, as is true of market and weather forecasting, neither of which has a stellar record. Moreover, all activities are subject to variation, as I have pointed out. If people don't understand this, then I suggest you turn in your project manager's hat for a better job.

Resource Availability

A major factor in dealing with resource allocation is the availability of each person to do project work. One guideline that industrial engineers follow is that no person is available to work more than 80 percent of the time. If you assume an eight-hour day, that means 6.4 hours a day available for work, and prudence says to just make it six hours. The 20 percent of lost availability goes to three factors called PFD. P means personal—every individual must take breaks. F is for fatigue—people lose productive time as they get tired. And D means delays—people lose time waiting for inputs from others, supplies, or instructions on what to do.

Experience shows, however, that the only people who are available to work even 80 percent of the time are those whose jobs tie them to their workstations. This is true for factory workers and others who do routine jobs like processing insurance claims (and even these people move around). With knowledge workers, you never get 80 percent of a day in productive work. The figure is usually closer to 50 percent, and it may be lower! One company that I know of did a time study in which people logged their time every hour for two weeks, and they found that project work accounted for only 25 percent of their time. The rest went to meetings, nonproject work that had to be done, old jobs that were finished long ago but came back to the person who originally worked on them, work on budgets for the next year, customer support, and on and on.

Most software programs allow you to specify the number of *working hours* needed for a task and the percentage of a day that a person will work on the task; the software then translates those estimates into calendar time. So, as an example, if a person is working on your project only half time and the task she is doing is supposed to take twenty hours of actual working time, then it will be a week (or more) before she finishes it.

It is especially important that you know the availability of people to do project work, or you will produce schedules that are worse than useless. I say worse because they will be misleadingly short, and they will wreak havoc with your organization. Do a time study to determine the number, then use it. And if people don't like the fact that a lot of time is being lost to nonproject activities, then correct the problem by removing those disruptive activities.

The usual solution is that people must work overtime to get their project work done because of all the disruptions that occur during the day. The problem is that studies have found that overtime has a very negative impact on productivity. So it is a losing battle. Short-term overtime is fine, but long spans just get organizations into trouble.

KEY POINTS TO REMEMBER

- You should ignore resource limitations when you begin developing a schedule. If two tasks can logically be done in parallel, draw them that way.
- The critical path is the one that is longest and has no float. Note that you can have a project on which the task with the longest path is not critical because it has float.

◆ Nobody is available to do productive work more than 80
   percent of a workday. You lose 20 percent to personal time,
   fatigue, and delays.

EXERCISE

For the network in figure 9-9, calculate the early and late times and
the float available on noncritical activities. Which activities form the
critical path? Answers are in the Answers section at the back of the
book.

[FIGURE 9-9]
NETWORK FOR EXERCISE

CHAPTER 10

PROJECT CONTROL AND EVALUATION

Every step taken up to now has been for one purpose: to achieve control of the project. This is what is expected of a project manager: that she manage organization resources in such a way that critical results are achieved.

However, there are two connotations to the word "control," and it is important that we use the one that is appropriate in today's world. One meaning of "control" refers to domination, power, and command. We control people and things through the use of that power. When we say, "Jump," people ask, "How high?" At least they used to. It doesn't work that well today.

I have previously discussed the fact that project managers often have a lot of responsibility but little authority. Let's examine that and see whether it is really a problem.

I have asked several corporate officers (presidents and vice presidents), "Since you have a lot of authority, does that authority guarantee that people will do what you want done?"

Uniformly, they answer, "No."

"What does get them to do what you want done?"

"Well, in the end analysis, they have to want to do it," they say.

"Then what does your authority do for you?" I ask.

"Well, it gives me the right to exercise sanctions over them, but that's all."

So we find that having authority is no guarantee that you will be able to get people to do your bidding. In the end, you have to get them to do it willingly, and that says you have to understand the motivations of people so that you can *influence* them to do what needs to be done. My son needed influencing to do his homework. He would often show me three-month-old homework, beautifully done, so he could go play video games. When I discovered the ruse, I had to determine what would motivate him to do it right, so I told my wife (I cannot discipline well). She took the Xbox away (influence) until he did his homework.

A second kind of authority has to do with taking actions unilaterally—that is, without having to get permission first. In this sense of the word, we *do* have a lot of organizational problems. I meet project managers who have project budgets in the millions of dollars (as much as $35 million in one case), yet who must have *all* expenditures approved. If a project plan and budget have been approved before the work was started and if the project manager is spending within the approved limits of the plan, why should she have to get more signatures for approved expenditures? Only if a deviation from the plan is going to result should more signatures be needed, and then the plan should be revised to reflect those changes.

....

There are two kinds of authority: One is power over people, and the other is the ability to make decisions and to act unilaterally.

....

Consider the messages being sent to these managers. On the one hand, they are being told, "We trust you to administer $35 million of our money." On the other hand, they are told, "But as you spend it, you must have every expenditure approved by someone of higher authority." One is a positive message: "We trust you." The other is negative. Which do you think comes through loud and clear? You bet! The negative.

A *negative* message *always* takes priority over a positive one.

Interestingly, we complain that people in organizations won't take more responsibility for themselves; then we treat them as though they are irresponsible and wonder why they don't behave responsibly!

So the first meaning of "control" has a power connotation. Another meaning is summed up by the following: *Control* is the act of comparing progress to the plan so that corrective action can be taken when a deviation from planned performance occurs. This definition implies the use of information as the primary ingredient of control rather than power. Thus, we talk about management information systems, and, indeed, these are the essence of what is needed to achieve control in projects.

Control: To compare progress against the plan so that corrective action can be taken when a deviation occurs.

Unfortunately, many organizations have management information systems that are good for tracking inventory, sales, and manufacturing labor but not for tracking projects. Where such systems are not in place, you will have to track progress manually.

Achieving Team Member Self-Control

Ultimately, the only way to control a project is for every member of the project team to be in control of his own work. A project manager can achieve control at the *macro* level only if it is achieved at the *micro* level. However, this does not mean that you should practice micromanaging! It actually means that you should set up conditions under which every team member can achieve control of his own efforts.

Doing this requires five basic conditions. To achieve self-control, team members need:

1. A clear definition of what they are supposed to be doing, with the purpose stated.
2. A personal plan for how to do the required work.
3. Skills and resources adequate to the task.
4. Feedback on progress that comes directly from the work itself.
5. A clear definition of their authority to take corrective action when there is a deviation from the plan (and it cannot be zero!).

The first requirement is that every team member be clear about what her objective is. Note the difference between tasks and objectives, which was discussed in chapter 5. State the objective and explain to the person (if necessary) the *purpose* of the objective. This allows the individual to pursue the objective in her own way.

The second requirement is for every team member to have a personal plan on how to do the required work. Remember, if you have no plan, you have no control. This must apply at the individual, as well as at the overall project level.

The third requirement is that the person have the skills and resources needed for the job. The need for resources is obvious, but this condition suggests that the person may have to be given training if she is lacking necessary skills. Certainly, when no employee is available with the required skills, it may be necessary to have team members trained.

The fourth requirement is that the person receive feedback on performance that goes directly to her. If such feedback goes through some roundabout way, she cannot exercise self-control. To make this clear, if a team member is building a wall, she must be able to measure the height of the wall, compare it to the planned performance, and know whether she is on track.

The fifth condition is that the individual must have a clear definition of her authority to take corrective action when there is a deviation from the plan, and it must be greater than zero authority! If she has to ask the project manager what to do every time a deviation occurs, the project manager is still controlling. Furthermore, if many people have to seek approval for every minor action, this puts a real burden on the project manager.

Characteristics of a Project Control System

The control system must focus on project objectives, with the aim of ensuring that the project mission is achieved. To do that, the control system should be designed with these questions in mind:

- What is important to the organization?
- What are we attempting to do?
- Which aspects of the work are most important to track and control?
- What are the critical points in the process at which controls should be placed?

Control should be exercised over what is important. On the other hand, what is controlled tends to become important. Thus, if budgets and schedules are emphasized to the exclusion of quality, only those will be controlled. The project may well come in on time and within budget but at the expense of quality. Project managers must monitor performance carefully to ensure that quality does not suffer.

Taking Corrective Action

A control system should focus on response: if control data do not result in action, then the system is ineffective. That is, if a control system does not use deviation data to *initiate corrective action*, it is not really a control system but simply a monitoring system. If you are driving and realize that you have somehow gotten on the wrong road but do nothing to get back on the right road, you are not exercising control.

One caution here, though. I once knew a manager whose response to a deviation was to go into the panic mode and begin micromanaging. He then got in the way of people trying to solve the problem and actually slowed them down. Had he left them alone, they would have solved their problem much faster.

Timeliness of Response

The response to control data must be timely. If action occurs too late, it will be ineffective. This is frequently a serious problem. Data on project status are sometimes delayed by four to six weeks, making them useless as a basis for taking corrective action. Ideally, information on project status should be available on a real-time basis. In most cases, that is not possible. For many projects, status reports that are prepared weekly are adequate.

Ultimately, you want to find out how many hours people *actually* work on your project and compare that figure to what was *planned* for them. This means that you want accurate data. In some cases, people fill out weekly time reports without having written down their working times daily. That results in a bunch of fiction, since most of us cannot remember with any accuracy what we did a week ago.

As difficult as it may be to do, you need to get people to record their working times daily so that the data will mean something when you collect them. What's in it for them? Perhaps nothing. Perhaps future estimates will be better as a result of your having collected accurate information on this project. In any case, you need accurate data, or you may as well not waste your time collecting them.

> When people fill out time reports weekly, without writing down what they did *daily*, they are making up fiction. Such made-up data are almost worse than no data at all.

When information collection is delayed for too long, the manager may end up making things worse instead of better. Lags in feedback systems are a favorite topic for systems theorists. The government's attempts to control recessions and inflation sometimes involve long delays, as a result of which the government winds up doing the exact opposite of what should have been done, thereby making the economic situation worse.

There is one point about control that is important to note. If every member of the project team is practicing proper control methods, then reports that are prepared weekly are just checks and balances. This is the desired condition.

Designing the Right System

One control system is not likely to be correct for all projects. It may need to be scaled down for small projects and beefed up for large ones. Generally, a control system adequate for a large project will overwhelm a small one with paperwork, while one that is good for small projects won't have enough clout for a big project.

Practicing the KISS Principle

KISS stands for "Keep it simple, stupid!" The smallest control effort that achieves the desired result should be used. Any control data that are not essential should be eliminated. However, as just mentioned, one common mistake is to try to control complex projects with systems that are *too simple*!

> "No problem is so big or so complicated that it can't
> be run away from."
> —CHARLIE BROWN (CHARLES SCHULTZ, *PEANUTS*)

To keep control simple, it is a good idea to check periodically that the reports generated are actually being used for something by the people who receive them. We sometimes create reports because we believe the information in them should be useful to others, but if the recipients don't actually use it, we are kidding ourselves. To test this point, send a memo with each report telling people to let you know whether they want to receive future reports; if you do not hear from them, their names will be removed from the distribution. You may be surprised to find that *no one* uses some of your reports. Those reports should be dropped completely.

Project Review Meetings

There are two aspects to project control. One can be called *maintenance*, and the other aims at *improvement* of performance. The maintenance review just tries to keep the project on track. The improvement review tries to help project teams improve performance. Three kinds of reviews are routinely conducted to achieve these purposes:

1. Status reviews
2. Process or lessons-learned reviews
3. Design reviews

Everyone should do status and process reviews. Design reviews, of course, are appropriate only if you are designing hardware, software, or some sort of campaign, such as a marketing campaign.

A status review is aimed at maintenance. It asks where the project stands on the PCTS measures that we have used throughout this book. Only if you know the value of all four of these can you be sure of where you are. This is the subject of chapter 12.

Process means the way something is done, and you can be sure that process always affects task performance; that is, how something is done affects the outcome. For that reason, process improvement is the work of every manager. How this is done is covered in the next section.

Project Evaluation

As the dictionary definition says, to evaluate a project is to attempt to determine whether the overall status of the work is acceptable in terms of intended value to the client once the job is finished. Project evaluation appraises the progress and performance of a job and compares them to what was originally planned. That evaluation provides the basis for management decisions on how to proceed with the project. The evaluation must be credible in the eyes of everyone affected, or decisions based on it will not be considered valid. The primary tool for project evaluation is the *project process review*, which is usually conducted at major milestones throughout the life of the project.

> **"Evaluate: to determine or judge the value or worth of."**
>
> —*THE RANDOM HOUSE DICTIONARY*

Purposes of Project Evaluation

Sports teams that practice without reviewing performance may get really *good* at playing very *badly*. That is why they review game films—to see where they need to improve. In other words, the purpose of a review is to learn lessons that can help the team to avoid doing things that cause undesired outcomes and to continue doing those that help. The review should be called a *lessons-learned*, or *process, review*.

I have deliberately avoided the word "audit" because nobody likes to be audited. Historically, an audit has been designed to catch people doing things they shouldn't have done so that they can be penalized in some way. If you go around auditing people, you can be sure they will hide from you anything they don't want you to know, and it is those very things that could help the company learn and grow.

As Dr. W. Edwards Deming has pointed out, there are two kinds of organizations in this world today: those that are getting better and those that are dying. An organization that stands still is dying. It just doesn't know it yet.

The reason? The competition is not sitting by idly. It is doing new things, some of which may be better than what you are doing. If you aren't improving, you will be passed by, and soon you won't have a market.

The same is true of every part of an organization. You can't suboptimize, improving just manufacturing. You have to improve every department, and that includes how you run projects.

In fact, good project management can give you a real competitive advantage, especially in product development. If you are sloppy in managing your projects, you don't have good control of development costs. That means that you have to either sell a lot of product or charge large margins to cover your development costs so that the project is worth doing in the first place. If you can't sell a lot of widgets, then you have to charge the large margin.

....
Good management of projects can give you a competitive advantage.
....

If your competitor, on the other hand, has good cost control, it can charge smaller margins and still be sure that it recovers its investment and makes money. Thus, it has a competitive advantage over you because of its better *control* of project work.

Additionally, in order to learn, people require feedback, like that gained by a team from reviewing game films. The last phase of a project should be a final process review, conducted so that the management of projects can be improved. However, such a process review should not be conducted only at the end of the project. Rather, process reviews should be done at major milestones in the project or every three months, whichever comes first, so that learning can take place as the job progresses. Furthermore, if a project is getting into serious trouble, the process review should reveal the difficulty so that a decision can be made to continue or terminate the work (see chapter 16).

> **In order to learn, we must have *feedback*.**
> **Furthermore, we tend to learn more from mistakes**
> **than from successes, painful though that may be**
> **to admit.**

Following are some of the general reasons for conducting periodic project process reviews. You should be able to:

- Improve project performance together with the management of the project.
- Ensure that quality of project work does not take a back seat to schedule and cost concerns.
- Reveal developing problems early so that action can be taken to deal with them.
- Identify areas where other projects (current or future) should be managed differently.
- Keep client(s) informed of project status. This can also help ensure that the completed project will meet the needs of the client.

- Reaffirm the organization's commitment to the project for the benefit of project team members.

Conducting the Project Process Review

Ideally, a project process review should be conducted by an independent examiner, who can remain objective in the assessment of information. The process review must be conducted in a spirit of learning rather than in a climate of blame and punishment. If people are afraid that they will be "strung up" for problems, then they will hide those problems if at all possible.

....

Process reviews conducted as witch hunts will produce witches.

....

Openness is hard to achieve. In many organizations, the climate has been punitive for so long that people are reluctant to reveal any less-than-perfect aspects of project performance. Dr. Chris Argyris, in his book *Overcoming Organizational Defenses: Facilitating Organizational Learning*, has described the processes by which organizations continue ineffective practices. All of them are intended to help individuals "save face" or avoid embarrassment. In the end, they also prevent organizational learning.

Two questions should be asked in the review. The first is, "What have we done well so far?" The second is, "What do we want to improve (or do better) in the future?" Notice that I am not asking, "What have we done badly?" That question serves only to make everyone defensive because people will assume that you will punish them for things done wrong. Furthermore, there is always the possibility that nothing has been done wrong, but there is always room to improve.

Finally, the results of the review should be published. Otherwise, the only people in the organization who can take advantage of it are the members of the team just reviewed. If other teams know what was learned, then they can benefit from that information. In the next section, we look at what the report should contain.

The Process Review Report

A company may decide to conduct process reviews in varying degrees of thoroughness, from totally comprehensive, to partial, to less formal and cursory. A formal, comprehensive process review should be followed by a report. The report should contain, at a minimum, the following:

- *Current Project Status.* The best way to do this is to use earned value analysis, as presented in chapter 12. However, when earned value analysis is not used, the current status should still be reported as accurately as possible.
- *Future Status.* This is a forecast of what is expected to happen in the project. Are significant deviations expected in schedule, cost, performance, or scope? If so, the report should specify the nature of the changes.
- *Status of Critical Tasks.* The report should describe the status of critical tasks, particularly those on the critical path. Tasks that have high levels of technical risk should be given special attention, as should those being performed by outside vendors or subcontractors, over which the project manager may have limited control.
- *Risk Assessment.* The report should mention any identified risks that could lead to monetary loss, project failure, or other liabilities.
- *Information Relevant to Other Projects.* The report should describe what has been learned from this process review that can or should be applied to other projects, whether in progress or about to start.
- *Limitations of the Process Review.* The report should mention any factors that may limit the validity of the process review. Are any assumptions suspect? Are any data missing or perhaps

contaminated? Was anyone uncooperative in providing information for the process review?

As a general comment, the simpler and more straightforward a project process review report, the better. The information should be organized so that both planned and actual results can be easily compared. Significant deviations should be highlighted and explained.

KEY POINTS TO REMEMBER

- The meaning of control that is important to project managers is the one that concerns the use of information, comparing actual progress to the plan so that action can be taken to correct for deviations from the plan.
- The only way a project is really under control is if all team members are in control of their own work.
- The effort used to control a project should be worthwhile. You don't want to spend $100 to purchase a $3 battery, for example.
- If you take no action in response to a deviation, you have a *monitoring* system, not a *control* system.
- Project working times must be recorded daily. If people wait a week to capture what they have done, they rely on memory and end up writing down *estimates* of what they did. Such data are no good for future estimating.
- Project evaluation is done to determine whether a project should continue or be canceled. Process reviews also should help the team learn in order to improve performance.

CHAPTER 11

THE CHANGE CONTROL PROCESS

The most comprehensive, effective project plan will be wasted if some method of controlling change is not implemented. Just as your diligence and ability to invest in planning directly affect project success or failure, so, too, does the establishment of a change control process. The *PMBOK® Guide*, seventh edition (p. 236), defines change as, "A modification to any formally controlled deliverable, project management plan component, or project document." Change has a direct effect on your project plan. If you do not keep the plan current, you have no plan. The original baseline plan (the foundation) will no longer be valid and will lose its effectiveness in dealing with current project scenarios.

Change control is not easy. It involves variables and judgment calls, thresholds and sign-offs. The change control process establishes the stability necessary for you to manage the multitude of changes that affect the project throughout its life cycle. If left unchecked, changes to the project plan cause significant imbalance regarding scope, schedule, and budget. The project manager who focuses on managing and controlling change develops a potent weapon to fight scope creep (see chapter 3). As changes occur, you will gain the ability to gauge their overall impact on the project and react accordingly.

> The change control process establishes the stability necessary for you to manage the multitude of changes that affect the project throughout its life cycle.

Change control cannot be accomplished in a vacuum. As you react and make adjustments, the project plan must be revised and distributed to predetermined stakeholders. These stakeholders are often identified in a project communication plan. In addition to stakeholder identification, the plan determines appropriate communication paths, levels of data dissemination, and general guidelines or protocols for the project team. This is an excellent example of how different elements of an overall project plan can complement one another. Typical stakeholders that should appear on the inform or distribution list are the project champion, team members, functional managers, support personnel, select external vendors, and legal. There can be other stakeholders involved as the project dictates.

Sources of Change

Change happens. As things mature and grow, changes occur naturally and are often healthy and welcome. Projects are no different. Issues arise, however, when changes occur and no corresponding assessment is made of their impact on the project, positive or negative. Sources of change can be many and varied, depending on the project. Think about the projects you are working on right now. What has caused you to modify your plan or make adjustments?

With some projects, the customer or an internal department may be driving the modifications. On others, changes can come from all possible directions. Figure 11-1 presents a visual illustration of this concept.

[FIGURE 11-1]
TRIPLE CONSTRAINTS TRIANGLE

As you can see, each side of the *triple constraints triangle* represents a key project constraint. Sources of change are generally associated with one or more sides of the triangle: scope, schedule, or budget. Project quality is a constant and should always be considered as a potential source and focus of change control. Scope changes should be identified as those that affect the project deliverable. As changes hit the triangle, it is your job to keep the triangle balanced by making necessary adjustments to your plan. If this is not accomplished, one or more sides of the triangle will become skewed and therefore imbalanced. Extra work will be required to complete the project successfully. Typical sources per the triangle include, but are not limited to, the following:

SCOPE
- Other projects are added due to consolidation.
- The client changes the requirements.

- Market conditions shift.
- Engineering encounters problems.

SCHEDULE
- The delivery date is accelerated.
- Competition pressures increase.
- The client requests early delivery.

BUDGET
- Management pulls 20 percent of the project budget.
- Raw material costs escalate.
- Project work requires the addition of a team member.

> **Sources of change are generally associated with one or more sides of the triple constraints triangle: *scope*, *schedule*, or *budget*.**

Understanding and identifying likely sources of change to your projects will assist you in remaining proactive. The change control process will require a decision as to whether to process the change request and then determine the most effective way to move forward. Some decisions are easy: the customer requests a legitimate design improvement, or the project champion deprioritizes the project and slips required delivery three months. But the project's fate dictates that many change requests require difficult assessments, analyses, and various approvals before the change can be processed. It is not always evident whether a specific change adds value or merely cosmetic adjustments to the project plan. The formal change control process really is your friend. As you will see in the next section, it helps guide you through the gray areas of change that often develop as the project matures.

The Six Steps in the Change Control Process

The change control process can vary but usually includes a number of important and mandatory steps. In this section, I outline six common steps that are found in a typical project change control process. Organizational culture, procedure, and project type directly affect how the steps are implemented. The project manager typically receives a change request from the requesting *entity* (individual/department/customer). At this point, it is important that you confirm the current version of the project plan. If the change is processed, its impact will be measured against the plan and adjustments will be made accordingly. *Keep the baseline current.*

- *Step 1: Enter the initial change control information into your change control log.*
  - Entering initial change control information into your change control log serves as the summary of all actions taken regarding changes requested and/or processed. A detailed change log can ultimately serve as a biography of the project as it matures (see figure 11-3 on page 170).
- *Step 2: Determine whether the change should be processed.*
  - By determining whether the change should be processed, you take on the role of the project's gatekeeper. All too often, I have seen project managers accept changes simply because they are requested. If the change doesn't make sense—if it doesn't add value or should not be processed for other reasons—push back. Request clarification or justification to help you arrive at a reasonable decision. If the change is rejected, log it and stop the process. If the change is accepted, begin assessing the impact to the project plan. This is typically done by asking this question: "How does the change affect the sides of my triangle: scope, schedule, and budget?"

- Quality, objective, and other elements of the project should also be considered when assessing impact. Prepare recommendations for implementation, and then complete the change control form.
- *Step 3: Submit recommendations to management and/or the customer for review and approval.*
  - Impact assessments should be submitted to management and/or your customer for review and approval. Other approvals should be obtained as necessary (i.e., functional department managers). Make appropriate modifications as comments are received from these stakeholders.
- *Step 4: Update the project plan.*
  - Don't forget to update the project plan! This can be and sometimes is forgotten in the frantic pace of the project environment. It is here that you will create a new project baseline. This will become the current plan.
- *Step 5: Distribute the updated plan.*
  - As previously mentioned, communication when the updated plan is distributed is critical. Use this step to ensure that all stakeholders are aware of the change and the adjusted baseline plan (for instance, revision 7). If the distribution list is incomplete, misalignment will occur between the project team and one or more of the stakeholders. Imagine your project team working on revision 3 while the California office is working on the original plan (this is actually a bad memory for me).
- *Step 6: Monitor the change and track progress against the revised plan.*
  - The impact of the change activity may be minor or severe, good or bad. Don't forget to check the project triangle to ensure that it remains balanced.

Organizational culture impacts how you establish the change control process and manage changes to your project. Be flexible.

I often ask my seminar attendees if they have an existing change control process to guide them; some do, but most don't. That reflects my own experience. When I moved from the defense industry (strong project processes) to the adult learning environment (less process), I needed to adjust. If you are faced with an environment where no change processes are in place, that is a good-news/bad-news scenario. The difficulty is in establishing change control while facing resistance to change, as well as general apathy. Nobody wants to sign anything, and there is little support in the decision-making process. Do it anyway! It is important for you to maintain control of the project through these changes. If a stakeholder or department manager signature cannot be obtained, write the department or stakeholder/manager name on the change control form and note the date. This is a control mechanism, not a "gotcha."

As project manager, it is your responsibility to fight scope creep and keep the triple constraints triangle balanced and under control. This is *your* tool for *your* project. The good news in the absence of any process is the absence of any process. You can set this up any way you like because there is nothing to replace. Yes, this will be time-consuming and a lot of work, but the payoff will be your process, your style.

For those who work in an environment with established change control procedures, use them. Quite often these procedures are designed to manage changes to the *product* (e.g., IT or R&D department), not the project. Make sure you take a holistic approach to change and focus on the project itself.

The Change Control Form

The *change control form* is the controlling document for the change process. This document is the project manager's tool for identifying, assessing, and, if necessary, processing changes that affect the project. In short, it keeps the project plan current. It should be filled out completely upon acceptance of the requested change. The data input is more than record keeping and requires analysis, estimation, and collaboration with team members, stakeholders, and subject matter experts. Without this form or a close proximity, there is no process because there is no control.

....

The change control form is the controlling document for the change process.

....

Figure 11-2 is a very comprehensive, detailed version of a change form. It is important that you review the form and adjust it to your own perceived requirements when managing changes as the project matures. You may need to streamline the template, or you may want to expand some portions. This is your call. If the document is too cumbersome, you will lose efficiency. If you simplify too much, key data will be lost.

Overview data are input at the top of the form, including project number, revision number, and date revised. I *always* include the objective statement on my change documents to ensure continuity and eliminate uncertainty. Change can breed uncertainty, and uncertainty is not your friend. As changes multiply on a typical project, include the original objective statement. This will keep stakeholders from wondering if the objective has changed because of the latest adjustments, or losing sight of the project objective entirely. If the impact is significant, a new objective statement may need to be agreed upon and communicated per the form. A brief description of the change is appropriate, and the reason should be included as well. In the mercurial project environment, it may be difficult—seven months and thirty-seven changes into the project—to recall why the team generated Change Order 2. Add the five other projects you might be managing to the scenario, and you can see how this added element of control can be helpful. *Reason for change* can also serve as a check on the system to ensure that value is added by implementing the change.

Schedule change information and estimated costs bring us back to the triple constraints triangle. It is crucial that you quantify the estimated impact of the change on both the project schedule and

[FIGURE 11-2]

PROJECT CHANGE CONTROL FORM

Project No.: 710 **Task No.:** 16 **Revision No.:** 1 **Date Revised:** 8/13/2021

Objective Statement:
Relocation of the accounting department to suitable and renovated quarters for 22 persons within the same building no later than December 31, 2021.

Description of Change:
Site #2 will not be available for evaluation until August 21 or 22. This will cause a two-day delay in the evaluation of all sites. This change will probably not cause a delay to the project but may delay the final site decision by one day.

Reason for Change:
The site will not be available for review and evaluation due to major corporate planning sessions that will consume that space for two days.

Schedule Change Information

Task No.	Task	Orig. Start Date	Orig. Comp. Date	New Start Date	New Comp. Date
16	Evaluate Site #2	8/15/21	8/20/21	8/17/21	8/22/21

Estimated Costs:

Approvals

Project Manager: Mr. Bill Boyd	**Date:** 8/11/21
Task Manager: Mr. Dan O'Brien	**Date:** 8/12/21
Functional Manager:	**Date:**
Senior Manager:	**Date:**

the budget. Some project managers prefer less detail than is shown in figure 11-2 and quantify the impact by noting the overall schedule delay or time saved. This is your call and is usually determined by style, organizational culture, project type, and so on. Sometimes, estimated costs are actual costs already realized or quotes received from vendors. Again, this will depend upon all of the variables associated with the change.

An effective change control form is obviously important for project control, but it can also come in handy.

A colleague of mine, a group program manager for the American Management Association International, was asked by a direct report managing a course revision project if she could colorize 25 percent of a *Train the Trainer* course book. He told her it was probably not a good idea because the production costs would be exorbitant. When she brought back a more reasonable request with appropriate approvals, the manager moved forward with the change, impacting the budget by about $10,000. At the subsequent steering committee review, he was asked about the budget increase. Expecting the question, he offered his next slide, a copy of the change request form, which two of the committee members had signed. He was able to proceed without needing an aspirin.

Thresholds

How much change is enough to trigger the process? Are there changes that are just not significant enough to justify filling out the form, acquiring signatures, and making other investments of time and effort? These are important questions for the project manager, and they offer an excellent time to consider thresholds. Most project processes require you to employ good project and business savvy. If the change is considered minor and the project plan can absorb the change with minimal impact, make the necessary adjustments and move on (see Example 1). If, however, a

severity threshold has been exceeded, this should trigger action by
you and your team to implement the change control process (see
Example 2).

....

**Are there changes that are just not significant enough
to justify filling out the form, acquiring signatures,
and making other investments of time and effort?**

....

Example 1:
If a $5 million project must endure a $10 change, it would be a
poor decision to trigger the process. A reasonable threshold might
be $1,000, depending upon budget constraints and industry
standards.

Example 2:
If your project deadline is four months from the date of the change
request and the estimated schedule delay is one week, the change
process should be triggered. Schedule thresholds require more
analysis based upon critical path implications (or not) and duration to complete. As always, you will need to take the temperature
of the project environment during the decision-making process.

   Because of the ever-changing environment that surrounds most
projects, thresholds are flexible, and you will often require input
from teammates or other stakeholders to determine the impact of
a change on the project. If you have done your homework and
invested time and effort in managing the previous project life-cycle
processes, you will be in a much better position to make informed
decisions regarding change.

The Change Control Log

As mentioned earlier in this chapter, the change control log enters
the picture in Step 1 of the change control process. As you might

expect, it is another control mechanism designed to identify proposed changes and track those accepted throughout the process.

Figure 11-3 is a template that you can use as presented or that you can streamline or expand as you deem necessary. In the absence of an organizational standard, I recommend that you adopt a singular, comprehensive approach to tracking changes across projects. You can add or omit information as appropriate.

[FIGURE 11-3]

PROJECT CHANGE CONTROL LOG

Change Number	Date of Change	Description of Change	Requested by	Status O/C	Schedule Impact	Budget Impact	Comments
1	8/12/21	Site #2 not available on 2/21	Jim Morrison		2 days	N/A	

As with many project templates, the concept is simple but not always easy to apply. Discipline is the key ingredient here. As changes, risks, and critical path issues are swirling about, you must be disciplined enough to stop what you are doing and work the log. Much of the information you input will seem self-evident or trivial, but the simplest detail may loom large as the project progresses. Change Number, Date of Change, and an abbreviated Description of Change are standard information. The approach used in figure 11-3 also includes columns for the requestor and status. There will be instances when a change will be accepted, but budget, schedule, technology, skill set, or something else presents a blockage to delay or even prevent implementation. I prefer O/C, open or closed, to identify status. You should then transfer Schedule Impact and Budget Impact from the change control form and update as necessary. Many project managers add a column for scope or objective impact prior to the final input that is reserved for comments or miscellaneous issues. Typical comments may concern stakeholder reluctance, technical problems, or remarks regarding other project issues.

> As changes, risks, and critical path issues are
> swirling about, you must be disciplined enough to
> stop what you are doing and work the log.

The Project Spin-Off

Think about some drastic changes that have affected your projects in the past. Sometimes project change, whatever the source, can be grounds for spinning off a new project while continuing with the original. Sometimes it is appropriate for the new project to simply replace the original due to skill-set requirements, location, budget demands, deprioritization, or a host of other reasons. There are also changes so severe that they justify closing the project down. When you get hit with the big one, it's often not easy and never fun. It doesn't even need to be one change; it may be an accumulation of changes that dramatically impacts the project. In any case, you need to have a firm grasp of the impact on the project and your recommendations moving forward. This can often be a sales job, and you will need to persuade with good data from the project plan.

> Sometimes project change, whatever the source, can
> be grounds for spinning off a new project while
> continuing with the original.

The project spin-off usually occurs when the change is so dramatic that you and your team determine that an entirely separate project should be initiated. This could be due to scope "explosion" or one or more of the many reasons previously detailed. If a new project moves forward with the existing one, it can often be managed in parallel, requiring coordination and alignment. If a new project manager takes over, it is probable that you will be called upon to coach her up to speed as the project life cycle is begun. It is in your best interest to do a thorough job here. Some of your team resources may be shared or transferred, depending upon the individual project circumstances.

> **The project spin-off usually occurs when the change is so dramatic that you and your team determine that an entirely separate project should be initiated.**

If the new project becomes a *satellite*, or subproject, the impact is far less drastic, and the new team will usually report directly to the original project manager. In contrast, if the new project replaces the old, you may just move on to other projects. In the event that it makes sense to keep you in place, manage the new project as you did the original. Begin at the beginning—*plan*. Then continue through the project life cycle as appropriate. It is important here to capture all of the work and data that can be useful moving forward on the new project. A careful analysis should be done to separate the wheat from the chaff. In some cases, skill-set requirements will require individual team members to be replaced. You may have to recruit an entirely new team, again depending on circumstances.

You may, as project manager, decide that the project should be *killed*; good luck. In my experience, it can be a difficult thing to do, but not impossible. If the project has lost its value, make your case. Use data, not emotion (see Chapter 16). The reasons can be many and varied, but if you have done your job, you will have the means to persuade with facts.

Embracing Change

Don't fear project change; embrace and manage it. This does not have to be a difficult task if you have invested yourself and the project team in establishing a formidable plan. As with scope creep, changes often represent necessary adjustments to the original project plan. It's how you manage these changes that makes all the difference and helps you deliver the project on time and on budget, with an excellent deliverable.

KEY POINTS TO REMEMBER

- Change must be controlled *and* communicated.
- Understanding and identifying likely sources of change assists you in remaining proactive. Typical sources of change are scope, schedule, and budget adjustments.
- It is crucial to keep the baseline plan current.
- The six common steps you will take in a typical change control process are to enter the initial change control information into your change control log; determine whether the change should be processed; submit recommendations to management and/or the customer for review and approval; update the project plan; distribute the updated plan; and monitor the change and track progress against the revised plan.
- The change control form and log are your primary controlling documents.
- Thresholds should be established when determining your response to project change.
- Project spin-off usually occurs when the project change is so dramatic that you and your team determine that an entirely separate project should be initiated.

EXERCISE

Identify a recent change to a project of yours that required a response. On the basis of what you've learned in this chapter, answer the following questions:

1. Is it appropriate to accept the change?
2. Should a change control document be triggered?
3. How did this change impact the project triangle?
4. To whom should the response be communicated?
5. What change thresholds are appropriate to establish for this project?

CHAPTER 12

PROJECT CONTROL USING EARNED VALUE ANALYSIS

ontrol is exercised to achieve project objectives, and we know that performance, cost, time, and scope targets are always important. Furthermore, we have seen that control is exercised by comparing performance to the plan and, when deviations or variances occur, taking corrective action to bring performance back on target.

As I said in chapter 10, the review that is concerned with maintenance or straightforward project control is the status review. This review asks where the project is in terms of all four PCTS variables. Each time progress is reviewed, you must ask these three questions:

1. Where are we (in terms of PCTS)?
2. When there is a deviation, what caused it?
3. What should be done about the deviation?

Note that only four actions can be taken in response to question 3:

1. Cancel the project.
2. Ignore the deviation.
3. Take corrective action to get back onto the planned progress.
4. Revise the plan to reflect a change in status that cannot be corrected.

Sometimes a project gets so far off track that it is no longer viable, and the best thing to do is to cancel it. Of course, this step is not taken lightly, but it should be taken in cases where you are just going to throw good money after bad. Cut your losses and get on with something better.

"Another day, another zero."

—ALFALFA (CARL SWITZER),
OUR GANG COMEDY SERIES

As for ignoring a deviation, if you can control to within a certain percentage tolerance and you are within those limits, you should usually ignore a deviation unless it shows a trend that will definitely take it outside the limits eventually. Otherwise, tweaking may just make the situation worse.

As for taking corrective action, there is no way to tell what this means, as it is specific to each project. Sometimes working people overtime gets a project back on track. Or perhaps you need to add people, or cut scope, or change the process. You must determine what must be done for your project.

In the event that the project is still viable but nothing can be done to get it back on track, you may have to revise the plan. Of course, you can also consider working overtime or reducing scope, since these were not originally called for. What I am really referring to here, however, is a situation in which you cannot recover, and you are revising the plan to show that the costs will increase, the deadline will slip, or some other change to the plan will occur.

Measuring Progress

One of the hardest things to do in managing projects is to actually *measure* progress. When you are following a road map, you monitor the road signs and see whether they agree with your planned route. In well-defined jobs, such as construction projects, it is generally fairly easy to tell where you are. You can measure the height of a brick wall or see whether all the conduit is installed, and so on. That is, you can tell where you are when a part of the work is actually *finished*. When work is poorly defined and it is only partially complete, however, you have to *estimate* where you are.

This is especially true of knowledge work—work done with one's head rather than with one's hands. If you are writing software code, designing something, or writing a book, it can be very hard to judge how far along you are and how much you have left to do.

Naturally, if you can't tell where you are, you can't exercise control. And note the use of the word "estimate" in measuring progress. What exactly is an estimate?

It's a guess.

And so we are guessing about where we are.

Yes. We'll know where we are when we get there. Until we actually arrive, we're guessing.

Does this not sound like something from *Alice in Wonderland*?

Heavens.

What was that definition of control again? Let's see—compare where you are . . .

How do you know where you are . . .

We're guessing.

. . . against where you are supposed to be. . . .

How do you know where you're supposed to be?

Oh, that's much easier. The plan tells us.

But where did the plan come from?

It was an estimate too.

Oh. So if one guess doesn't agree with the other guess, we're supposed to take corrective action to make the two of them agree, is that it?

That's what this guy says in his book.

Must be a book on witchcraft and magic.

Well, since it is impossible to know for sure where we are, then perhaps we should just give up on the whole thing and keep running projects by the seat of our pants. Right?

Wrong.

The fact that measures of progress are not very accurate does not justify the conclusion that they shouldn't be used. Remember, if you have no plan, you have no control, and if you don't try to monitor and follow the plan, you definitely don't have control. And if you have no control, there is no semblance of managing. You're just flailing around.

> The difficulty of measuring progress does not justify the conclusion that it shouldn't be done. You cannot have control unless you measure progress.

What is important to note, however, is that some projects are capable of tighter control than others. Well-defined work, which can be accurately measured, can be controlled to tight tolerances. Work that is more nebulous (e.g., knowledge work) has to allow larger tolerances. Management must recognize this and accept it. Otherwise, you go crazy trying to achieve 3 percent tolerances. It's like trying to push a noodle in a straight line or nail jelly to a wall.

Measuring Project Performance/Quality

If you think measuring progress is hard, try measuring quality. Were the bolts holding the steel beams together put in properly? Are all the welds sound? How do you tell?

This is the hardest variable to track, and one that often suffers as a consequence. Also, so much attention tends to be focused on cost and schedule performance that the quality of the work is often sacrificed. This can be a disaster, in some cases resulting in lawsuits against a company for damages that result from poor-quality work.

> **Work quality is most likely to be sacrificed when deadlines are tight. Constant attention is required to avoid this tendency.**

Project managers must pay special attention to the quality variable, in spite of the difficulty of tracking it.

Earned Value Analysis

It is one thing to meet a project deadline at any cost. It is another to do it for a *reasonable* cost. Project cost control is concerned with ensuring that projects stay within their budgets, while getting the work done on time and at the correct quality.

One system for doing this, called *earned value analysis*, was developed in the 1960s to allow the government to decide whether a contractor should receive a progress payment for work done. The method is finally coming into its own outside government projects, and it is considered the correct way to monitor and control almost any project. The method is also called, simply, *variance analysis*.

Variance analysis allows the project manager to determine trouble spots in the project and to take corrective action. The following definitions are useful in understanding the analysis:

- *Cost Variance.* Compares deviations and performed work.
- *Schedule Variance.* Compares planned and actual work completed.

- *BCWS* (*Budgeted Cost of Work Scheduled*). The budgeted cost of work scheduled to be done in a given time period or the level of effort that is supposed to be performed in that period.
- *BCWP* (*Budgeted Cost of Work Performed*). The budgeted cost of work actually performed in a given period or the budgeted level of effort actually expended. BCWP is also called *earned value* and is a measure of the dollar value of the work actually accomplished in the period being monitored.
- *ACWP* (*Actual Cost of Work Performed*). The amount of money (or effort) actually spent on completing work in a given period.

Variance thresholds can be established that define the level at which reports must be sent to various levels of management within an organization.

Cost variance = BCWP – ACWP
Schedule variance = BCWP – BCWS

Variance: any deviation from the plan.
By combining cost and schedule variances, an integrated cost/schedule reporting system can be developed.

Variance Analysis Using Spending Curves

Variances are often plotted using spending curves. A BCWS curve for a project is presented in figure 12-1. It shows the *cumulative spending* planned for a project and is sometimes called a *baseline plan*.

In the event that software is not available to provide the necessary data, figure 12-2 shows how data for the curve are generated. Consider a simple bar chart schedule. Only three tasks are involved. Task A involves forty labor-hours per week at an average loaded labor rate of $20 per hour, so that task costs $800 per week. Task B involves one hundred hours per week of labor at $30 per hour,

[FIGURE 12-1]

BCWS CURVE

[FIGURE 12-2]

BAR CHART SCHEDULE ILLUSTRATING CUMULATIVE SPENDING

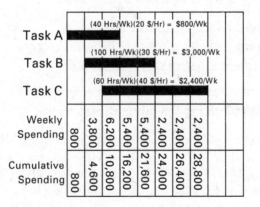

so it costs $3,000 per week. Finally, Task C spends $2,400 per week, assuming sixty hours per week of labor at $40 per hour.

At the bottom of the chart, we see that during the first week, $800 is spent for project labor; in the second week, both Tasks A and B are running, so the labor expenditure is $3,800. In the third week, all three tasks are running, so labor expenditure is the sum of the three, or $6,200. These are the *weekly* expenditures.

The *cumulative* expenditures are calculated by adding the cost for each subsequent week to the previous cumulative total. These cumulative amounts are plotted in figure 12-3. This is the spending curve for the project and is called a BCWS curve. Since it is derived directly from the schedule, it represents planned performance and therefore is called a baseline plan. Furthermore, since control is exercised by comparing progress to the plan, this curve can be used as the basis for such comparisons so that the project manager can tell the status of the program. The next section presents examples of how such assessments are made.

[FIGURE 12-3]

CUMULATIVE SPENDING FOR THE SAMPLE BAR CHART

Consider the curves shown in figure 12-4. On a given date, the project is supposed to have involved $40,000 (40K) in labor (BCWS). The actual cost of the work performed (ACWP) is 60K. These figures are usually obtained from accounting and are derived from all the time cards that have reported labor applied to the project. Finally, the budgeted cost of work performed (BCWP) is 40K. Under these conditions, the project would be behind schedule and overspent.

Figure 12-5 illustrates another scenario. The BCWP and the ACWP curves both fall at the same point, 60K. This means that the project is ahead of schedule but spending correctly for the amount of work done.

[FIGURE 12-4]

PLOT SHOWING PROJECT BEHIND SCHEDULE AND OVERSPENT

[FIGURE 12-5]

PROJECT AHEAD OF SCHEDULE, SPENDING CORRECTLY

The next set of curves illustrates another status. In figure 12-6, the BCWP and the ACWP curves are both at 40K. This means the project is behind schedule and under budget. However, because the manager spent 40K and got 40K of value for it, spending is correct for what has been done. There is a *schedule variance* but not a spending variance.

Figure 12-7 looks like figure 12-4, except that the ACWP and the BCWP curves have been reversed. Now the project is ahead of schedule and underspent.

[FIGURE 12-6]

PROJECT IS BEHIND SCHEDULE BUT SPENDING CORRECTLY

The relationships of P, T, C, and S

Variance Analysis Using Hours Only

In some organizations, project managers are held accountable not for costs but only for the hours actually worked on the project and for the work actually accomplished. In this case, the same analysis can be conducted by stripping the dollars off the figures. This results in the following:

- BCWS becomes total planned (or scheduled) hours.
- BCWP becomes Earned Hours (scheduled hours × percentage work accomplished).
- ACWP becomes Actual Hours Worked.

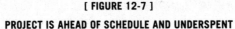

[FIGURE 12-7]

PROJECT IS AHEAD OF SCHEDULE AND UNDERSPENT

cv = cost variance   - - - - - **ACWP**
sv = schedule variance   .... **BCWP**

Using hours only, the formulas become:

Schedule Variance = BCWP – BCWS =
Earned Hours – Planned Hours

Labor Variance = BCWP – ACWP =
Earned Hours – Actual Hours Worked

Tracking hours only does lead to one loss of sensitivity. ACWP is actually the composite of a labor rate variance times a labor-hours variance. When only labor-hours are tracked, you have no warning that labor rates might cause a project budget problem. Nevertheless, this method does simplify the analysis and presumably tracks the project manager only on what she can control.

Responding to Variances

It is not enough to simply detect a variance. The next step is to understand what it means and what caused it. Then you have to decide what to do to correct for the deviation. Earlier, I explained that four responses can be made when there is a deviation from the plan. Which of these you choose depends in part on what caused the deviation. Following are some general guidelines:

- When ACWP and BCWP are almost equal and larger than BCWS (see figure 12-5), it usually means that extra resources have been applied to the project but at the labor rates originally anticipated. This can happen in several ways. Perhaps you planned for weather delays, but the weather has been good and you have gotten more work done during the analysis period than intended but at the correct cost. Thus, you are ahead of schedule but spending correctly.

- When ACWP and BCWP are nearly equal and below BCWS (see figure 12-6), it usually means the opposite of the previous situation; that is, you have not applied enough resources. Perhaps they were stolen from you, perhaps it has rained more than you expected, or perhaps everyone has decided to take a vacation at once. The problem with being in this position is that it usually results in an overspend when you try to catch up.

- When ACWP is below BCWS and BCWP is above BCWS (see figure 12-7), you are ahead of schedule and underspent. This generally happens because the original estimate was too conservative (probably padded for safety). Another possibility is that you had a lucky break. You thought the work would be harder than it was, so you were able to get ahead. Sometimes it happens because people were much more efficient than expected. The problem with this variance is that it ties up resources that could be used on other projects. The economists call this an *opportunity cost*. There is also a good chance that if you were consistently padding estimates and were bidding against other companies on projects, you probably lost some bids. If your competitor is using average values for time estimates while you are padding yours, then your figures are likely to be higher, and you will lose the bid.

Acceptable Variances

What are *acceptable variances*? The only answer that can be given to this question is, "It all depends." If you are doing a well-defined construction job, the variances can be in the range of +3–5 percent. If the job is research and development, acceptable variances increase generally to around +10–15 percent. When the job is pure research, the sky is the limit. Imagine, for example, that you worked for a pharmaceutical company and your boss said, "Tell me how long it will take and how much it will cost for you to discover and develop a cure for coronavirus and all variants."

For every organization, you have to develop tolerances through experience. Then you start trying to reduce them. All progress is an attempt to reduce variation in what we do. We will never reduce it to zero unless we eliminate the process altogether, but zero has to be the target.

Using Percentage Complete to Measure Progress

The most common way to measure progress is to simply estimate percentage complete. This is the BCWP measure, but BCWP is expressed as a dollar value, whereas *percentage complete* does not make that conversion.

When percentage complete measures are plotted over time, you tend to get a curve like the one shown in figure 12-8. It rises more or less linearly up to about 80 or 90 percent, then turns horizontal (meaning that no further progress is being made). It stays there for a while; then, all of a sudden, the work is completed.

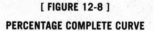

[FIGURE 12-8]

PERCENTAGE COMPLETE CURVE

The reason is that problems are often encountered near the end of the task, and a lot of effort goes into trying to solve them. During that time, no progress is made.

Another part of the problem is in knowing where you are to begin with. We have already said that you are generally estimating progress. Consider a task that has a ten-week duration. If you ask the person doing that task where he is at the end of the first week, he is likely to tell you, "10 percent"; at the end of week two, "20 percent"; and so on. What he is doing is making a *reverse inference.* It goes like this: "It is the end of the first week on a ten-week task, so I must be 10 percent complete." The truth is, he really doesn't know where he is. Naturally, under such conditions, control is very loose. Still, this is the only way progress can be measured in many cases.

KEY POINTS TO REMEMBER

- Control is exercised by analyzing the plan.
- Well-defined projects can achieve tighter control over variations than poorly defined ones.
- There is a tendency to sacrifice quality when deadlines are difficult to meet.
- It is not enough to recognize a variance. Its cause must be determined so that corrective action can be taken.
- Acceptable variances can be determined only through experience. Every system has a capability. Your team may have the ability to maintain better tolerances on their work than another team.

EXERCISE

Consider the report in figure 12-9, showing earned value figures for a project. Answer the questions by analyzing the data. Answers are provided in the Answers section at the back of the book.

1. Is the task ahead or behind schedule? By how much?
2. Is the task overspent or underspent? By how much?
3. When the task is completed, will it be overspent or underspent?

[FIGURE 12-9]
EARNED VALUE REPORT

WBS #	Cumulative-to-date			Variance		At Completion		
	BCWS	BCWP	ACWP	SCHED.	COST	BUDGET	L. EST.	VARIANCE
301	800	640	880	−160	−240	2,400	2,816	−416

CHAPTER 13

MANAGING THE PROJECT TEAM

T he previous chapters have concentrated primarily on the tools of project management—how to plan, schedule, and control the work. Unfortunately, far too many project managers see these tools as all they need to manage successfully. They assemble a team, give the members their instructions, and then sit back and watch the project self-destruct. Then they question whether there might be some flaw in the tools.

In all likelihood, the problem was with how people were managed. Even in those cases where a problem with the tools may have existed, it is often the failure of people to properly apply them that causes the problem, so, again, we are back to people.

The tools and techniques of project management are a *necessary* but not a *sufficient* condition for project success. As I have stated, if you can't handle people, you will have difficulty managing projects, especially when the people don't "belong" to you.

Related to this is the need to turn a project *group* into a *team*. Far too little attention is paid to team building in project management. This chapter offers some suggestions on how to go about it.

Team Building

Building an effective team begins on the first day of the team's existence. Failure to begin the team-building process may result in a team that is more like a group than a team. In a group, members may be *involved* in but not *committed* to the activities of the majority.

....
Teams don't just happen—they must be *built*!
....

The problem of commitment is a major one for both organizations and project teams. It is especially significant in matrix organizations, in which members of the project team are actually members of functional groups and have their own bosses but report to the project manager on a "dotted-line" basis.

Later in this chapter, I present rules for how a project manager can develop commitment to a team. For now, let us turn to how to get a team organized so that it gets off to the right start. [For an in-depth treatment of this topic, see *Project Team Leadership and Communication,* Samuel A. Malachowsky, PMP (Lintwood Press, 2018).]

Promoting Teamwork Through Planning

A primary rule of planning is that those individuals who must implement the plan should participate in preparing it. Yet leaders often plan projects by themselves, then wonder why their team members seem to have no commitment to the plans.

All planning requires some estimating—how long a task will take, given the availability of certain resources, and so on. In my seminars, I ask participants, "Do you often find that your boss thinks you can do your work much faster than you actually can?" They laugh and agree. As I tell them, it seems to be some kind of psychological law that bosses are optimistic about how long it will take their staff to get jobs done.

When a manager gives a person an assignment that allows inadequate time to be done, the individual naturally feels discouraged, and her commitment is likely to suffer. She might say, "I'll give it my best shot," but her heart isn't really in it.

Getting Organized

Here are the four major steps in organizing a project team:

1. Decide what must be done, using work breakdown structures, problem definitions, and other planning tools.
2. Determine staffing requirements to accomplish the tasks identified in the first step.
3. Recruit members for the project team.
4. Complete your project plan with the participation of team members.

Recruiting

Following are some of the criteria by which team members should be selected:

- The candidate possesses the skills necessary to perform the required work at the speed needed to meet deadlines.
- The candidate will have his needs met through participation in the project (see the March and Simon rules discussed in "Developing Commitment to a Team" later in this chapter).
- The applicant has the temperament to fit in with other team members who have already been recruited and with the project manager and other key players.
- The person will not object to overtime requirements, tight timetables, or other project work requirements.

Clarifying the Team's Mission, Goals, and Objectives

Peters and Waterman, in their book *In Search of Excellence* (Harper Business, 2006), have said that excellent organizations "stick to their knitting." They stick to what they are good at and do not go off on tangents, trying to do something they know nothing about. (Imagine, as an example, a hockey team deciding to play basketball.)

Numerous case studies and articles have been written about organizations that went off on tangents, at great cost, because they forgot their mission. The same can happen to project teams. If members are not clear on the team's mission, they will take the team where they think it is supposed to go, and that may not be the direction intended by the organization. The procedure for developing a mission statement is covered in chapter 5, so no more will be said about it here. However, working with your team to develop a mission statement is a good team-building activity in itself.

> If possible, the *entire team* should participate in developing the team's mission statement. This is a tremendous *team-building activity* in itself!

Conflicts Between Individual Goals and the Team's Mission

Experience has shown that team members are most committed to a team when their individual needs are being met. Sometimes members have what are called *hidden agendas*, personal objectives that they do not want anyone to know about because they are afraid other members will try to block them if their objectives are known. Since a manager should try to help individual members achieve their personal goals while achieving team goals as well, the team leader needs to bring hidden agendas into the open so that each individual can be helped to achieve his goal. Of course, a person may occasionally have a goal that runs so counter to the team's goals that no reconciliation is possible. In that case, if the team leader can discover the person's goal, the individual can (ideally) be moved to another team in which his goal can be reached.

> A manager should try to satisfy the needs of the
> organization, while *simultaneously* helping
> individuals satisfy their own needs through
> participation in the project.

Team Issues

A team must deal with four general issues: *goals, roles and responsibilities, procedures,* and *relationships.* In this chapter, we have dealt with clarifying the team's mission, goals, and objectives. This is *always* the first and most important step in developing a team.

> Every team must deal with:
>
> - Goals
> - Roles and responsibilities
> - Procedures
> - Relationships

Once that is done, people must understand their roles. These must be clearly defined. *What is expected* of each individual, and *by when?* The one problem that seems common is that team leaders think they clearly communicate this information to team members. Yet when you ask team members if they are clear on their goals and roles, you frequently get a negative response.

The problem is with our failure to solicit feedback from team members in order to be sure that they understood; in addition, members themselves are sometimes reluctant to admit that they

haven't understood. This appears to be a result of our tendency in
school to put people down for asking "stupid questions." So,
rather than admit that they don't understand, they *interpret* what
they have been told and try to do the job the best they can.

Project leaders must establish a climate of open communication
with the team in which no one feels intimidated about speaking
up. The best way to do this is to comment on the problem: "I
know some of you may feel reluctant to speak up and say you
don't understand, but we can't operate that way. Please feel free to
be candid. If you don't understand, say so. If you don't agree with
something, say so. That is the only way we can succeed. We will
be lucky to have time to do the job once, much less find time to
do it over because one of you failed to understand what was
expected."

> There is no such thing as a *stupid question*—except
> perhaps the one you were afraid to ask.

I have also found that people respond very positively when I am
willing to admit that I don't understand something myself or am
apprehensive or concerned about a project issue. If you project an
air of infallibility, no one else is likely to admit a weakness. But
then, who wants to deal with a demigod? A little human frailty
goes a long way toward breaking down barriers. I know this con-
tradicts what some managers have been taught. The macho notion
of infallibility has been with us for a long time, and I believe it is
the cause of many of our organizational problems. It is time to
abandon it for reality.

Working Out Procedures

Dealing with *how we do it* comes next. The key word here is "processes." The work must be done as efficiently and as effectively as
possible, and improvement of work processes is a very important

issue today. It is commonly called *re-engineering* and is the analysis and improvement of work processes to make the organization more competitive.

The difficulty that most teams have with process is that they get so focused on doing the work that they forget to examine how it is done. Periodically, a team should stop working long enough to examine its processes and to see whether it could use better approaches. Otherwise, the team may get very good at doing the work badly.

Relationships in Teams

Friction occurs in nearly every interaction between human beings. There are misunderstandings, conflicts, personality clashes, and petty jealousies. Project managers must be prepared to deal with these. In fact, if you really dislike having to deal with the behavioral problems that occur on projects, you should ask yourself whether you really want to manage projects at all. Like it or not, the behavioral problems come with the job, and failure to deal with them will sink a project eventually.

One thing to be aware of is that many personality clashes are the result of people's lack of good interpersonal skills. Some may have never been taught how to sit down and work out differences with others, so when the inevitable conflict happens, the situation just blows up. The best way to minimize the impact of such problems is to provide training for all team members (including yourself) in interpersonal skills. This area has been sorely neglected in many organizations because there seems to be no bottom-line impact. It is hard to demonstrate that there will be a $10 return on a $1 training investment.

Because of our inability to quantify the benefits of skills training, we don't provide it. Yet if we have capital resources that don't work well, we spend whatever is necessary to correct the problem. Interestingly, our *human resources* are the only ones that are renewable almost indefinitely, but we fail to take steps to keep them functioning effectively. As a project manager, you owe it to yourself to manage this aspect of the job.

> So-called personality conflicts are often simply the result of people's lack of good interpersonal skills. This lack can be resolved through training.

Stages in a Team's Development

A number of models describe the stages that teams or groups go through on the way to maturity. One of the more popular ones has self-explanatory titles for the stages: *forming, storming, norming,* and *performing.*

> The most popular terms for the stages of team development are:
>
> * Forming
> * Storming
> * Norming
> * Performing

In the *forming* stage, people are concerned with how they will fit in and with who calls the shots, makes decisions, and so on. During this stage, they look to the leader (or someone else) to give them some *structure*—that is, to give them a sense of direction and to help them get started. A leader's failure to do this may result in loss of the team to some member who exercises what we call *informal leadership.*

The *storming* stage is frustrating for most people. When the team reaches this stage, people begin to question their goals. Are they on the right track? Is the leader really leading them? They sometimes play *shoot the leader* during this stage.

At the *norming* stage, they are beginning to resolve their conflicts and to settle down to work. They have developed *norms* (unwritten rules) about how they will work together, and they feel more comfortable with one another. Each individual has found her place in the team and knows what to expect of the others.

Finally, when the team reaches the *performing* stage, the leader's job is easier. Members generally work well together now, enjoy doing so, and tend to produce high-quality results. In other words, we can really call them a team at this point.

Leading a Team Through the Stages

A newly formed team needs considerable structure, or it will not be able to get started. As I noted in the previous section, a leader who fails to provide such structure during Stage 1, the forming stage, may be rejected by the group, which will then look for leadership from someone else. A *directive* style of leadership is called for in the *forming* stage.

> A *directive* style of leadership is called for when a team is in the *forming* stage.

During this stage, members also want to get to know one another and want to understand the role each member will play on the team. In Stage 1, the leader must help team members get to know one another and help them become clear on goals, roles, and responsibilities. Leaders who are very task-oriented tend to make a major error here: They just tell the team to "get to work," without helping members get to know one another. They view such purely "social" activities as a waste of time; surely members can attend to such things themselves. Although it seems obvious, it is hard to see yourself as a team when you don't know some of the players.

Getting the team started with a kickoff party or dinner is one way to let members become acquainted in a purely social way, with no pressure to perform actual task work. If this is not feasible, there must be some mechanism for letting people get to know one another.

As the group continues to develop, it enters Stage 2, *storming*. Here, people are beginning to have some anxiety. They start to question the group's goal: Are we doing what we're supposed to be doing? The leader must use *influence* or *persuasion* to assure them that they are indeed on track. They need a lot of psychological support, as well. They must be assured by the leader that they are valued, that they are vital to the success of the team, and so on. In other words, members need some stroking in this stage.

> A *selling*, or *influence*, style of leadership is appropriate at the *storming* stage.

There is a tendency to try to skip this stage, as managers feel uncomfortable with the conflict that occurs. To sweep such conflict under the rug and pretend that it doesn't exist is a mistake. The conflict must be *managed* so that it does not become destructive, but it must not be avoided. If it is, the group will keep coming back to this stage to try to resolve the conflict, and this will inhibit progress. Better to pay now and get it over with.

As the team enters Stage 3, *norming*, it is becoming closer knit. Members are beginning to see themselves as a team and take some sense of personal identity from membership in the group. Members are now involved in the work, are becoming supportive of one another, and, because of their cooperation, can be said to be more of a team than a group at this point. The leader needs to adopt a *participative* style in this stage and share decision making more than in Stages 1 and 2.

In the *norming* stage, the leader should adopt a
participative style of leadership.

By the time a group reaches Stage 4, *performing*, it is a real team. The leader can generally sit back and concentrate on what-if analysis of team progress, planning for future work, and so on. This is a *delegative* style of leadership and is appropriate. The team is achieving results, and members are usually taking pride in their accomplishments. In this stage, there should be signs of camaraderie, joking around, and real enjoyment in working together.

Delegative leadership is the proper style in the
performing stage of a team's development. Note
that *delegation* does not mean abdication!

It is important to remember that no team stays in a single stage forever. If it encounters obstacles, it may drop back to Stage 3, and the leader can no longer be delegative but must back up to the Stage 3 management style, which is participative.

Membership in project teams often changes. When new members come on board, you should consider that for a short time the team will fall back to Stage 1, and you will have to take it back through the stages until it reaches maturity again. It is *especially* important that you help everyone get to know the new member and understand what his role will be in the team. This does take some time, but it is essential if you want the team to progress properly.

Developing Commitment to a Team

At the beginning of this chapter, I pointed out that helping team members develop commitment to the project is a major problem for project managers. Team members are often assigned to a project simply because they are the best *available* people, not because they are the best people for the job. When this happens, they may have no commitment to the team.

In their book *Organizations* (Blackwell, 2nd ed. 1993), March and Simon present five rules for developing commitment to a team or organization:

1. Have team members interact frequently so that they gain a sense of being a team.
2. Be sure that individual needs are being met through participation in the team.
3. Let all members know why the project is important. People don't like working on a "loser."
4. Make sure all members share the goals of the team. One bad apple can spoil the barrel.
5. Keep competition within the team to a minimum. Competition and cooperation are opposites. Let members compete with people outside the team, not within it.

Note that the first rule cannot always be followed if the team is scattered geographically. In that case, members should meet frequently through teleconferencing, videoconferencing, Zoom, or one of the many other virtual tools offered today (see chapter 14). It is almost impossible to think of yourself as part of a team if the team never gets together in some manner.

A Final Suggestion

If you want some good models of how to work with teams, take a look at the best coaches and see how they do it. Be careful, though, not to model the supermacho coach's behavior. That might work okay with a sports team, where people are there because they want to be there, but it is unlikely to work well with a project team where the members are there because they have to be. I also suggest that you watch the movie *Stand and Deliver* and see how Jaime Escalante deals with his kids. Then, the next time you are tempted to complain that you have a lot of responsibility and no authority, ask yourself how a teacher (who has even less authority than you do) can get a bunch of kids to work so hard. How did he get them to go to summer school or take math two periods a day? Then you will begin to realize what true leadership is all about.

KEY POINTS TO REMEMBER

- Teams don't just happen—they must be built!
- Having the entire team participate in planning is one way to start the team-building process.
- Deal with *goals*, *roles and responsibilities*, *procedures*, and *relationships*, in that order.
- So-called personality conflicts are often caused by team members' poor interpersonal skills. For teams to function well, *all* members should receive training in this area.
- The style of leadership appropriate for a team depends on its stage of development. In the *forming* stage, it is directive. In *storming,* it is influencing. At the *norming* stage, switch to a participative style. Finally, when the team reaches the *performing* stage, you can be delegative.

CHAPTER 14

THE PROJECT MANAGER AS LEADER

You must take an art and discipline approach in the project environment when leading your project team: the art of managing people and the discipline of applying the necessary project processes to be successful. I hear it all the time because it is true. It has been my experience that the people factor can be and often is the most challenging part of the project equation. The project champion, team members, functional managers, subject matter experts, and virtually all stakeholders need to be effectively managed to ensure project success. Chapters 1 and 2 introduced definitions of generic leadership, and chapter 13 related leadership style to the stages of project team development. Now I'm going to focus on what it means to be a project leader, understanding strengths and weaknesses, creating constituents, and understanding the importance of motivation. I will also discuss conflict resolution, team synergies, and a practical approach to *leading* project meetings (not managing them).

Laying the Foundation

Before you can attempt to understand and lead others, you should invest in a meaningful self-inventory. I am not suggesting days of psychoanalysis but a practical look in the mirror at your own behavior and probable *drivers* of this behavior. This typically provides valuable insight regarding your actions, as well as those of your team members and other project stakeholders.

Understanding Leadership Characteristics

When leading project management seminars, I often ask the attendees to raise their hands if they have extra time on any given day. It is a rhetorical question, asked to emphasize the need to maximize every interaction. Given the frantic pace of the project environment, almost every encounter can be considered critical. An improved understanding of yourself and your stakeholders will lead to more efficient communication and better project leadership decisions. Your ability to persuade, motivate, and resolve conflicts will improve. When you *lay the foundation* regarding these people skills, you avoid behavioral misalignment with stakeholders on all levels. Your understanding of leadership characteristics—individual traits, strengths, and weaknesses—indicates how you should flex your style and adjust to the stakeholder and the situation. This produces better overall alignment, which leads to greater efficiency. In terms of best practice, the more *agile* you become, the greater the chance for project success.

> **An improved understanding of yourself and your stakeholders will lead to more efficient communication and better project leadership decisions.**

Understanding Leadership Styles

I have seen many projects fail because the project manager insists that stakeholders adjust to the leader's style. As mentioned earlier, project team maturation requires you to progress from the directive leadership style to the delegative approach. This is logical and applies to most team scenarios, emphasizing the need for flexibility in your approach. As you move through a typical project day, however, you are faced with many and varied interactions, which require a smooth transition from one leadership style to the next. Some project leaders possess a natural aptitude for this, whereas others need to work at it. You should invest time and effort in developing this skill. Just as a chameleon changes skin color to maximize survival, so should you adjust your approach to people, situations, and circumstances to ensure project efficiency.

> **Just as a chameleon changes skin color to maximize survival, so should you adjust your approach to people, situations, and circumstances to ensure project efficiency.**

Most of us have a natural preferred style that we are comfortable with, aptly named the comfort zone. This can often make the transition from project manager to leader difficult to begin with. It is easy for you to operate when you are behaving naturally. When circumstances require you to break out of this area, though, it requires a certain amount of work. To be an effective project leader, you should be cognizant of the reluctance you will probably encounter when changing your own behavior. If the directive style is indicated when dealing with a stakeholder and it happens to be your least preferred, make a conscious effort to be disciplined and nimble enough to modify your preferred approach and be direct. All of this attention to project leadership detail will result in improved alignment among your leadership style, your stakeholder's behavioral characteristics, and the numerous project scenarios encountered on a daily basis. Figure 14-1 presents a good visual context of this alignment.

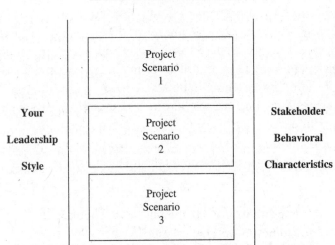

[FIGURE 14-1]

LEADERSHIP STYLE AND ALIGNMENT

Creating Project Constituents

In the late twentieth century, very little attention was paid to the concept of project manager as leader. In a typical status meeting, team members reported progress regarding assigned action items (the same as today). If the work was not completed, the team member was often singled out, or perhaps his functional manager was called. Turnover was commonplace in the project team environment.

Times have changed. Effective project leadership is recognized by colleges, practitioners, and, yes, authors, as an integral part of overall project success. The rise of project-based organizations (in which most work is accomplished through projects), the virtual nature and reach of global projects, and cultural diversity have all contributed to the demand for better leaders, not just managers of teams. Leaders need constituents, and project leaders are no exception.

Creating a Consistency in Working Relationships

To create a *constistency*, team members and stakeholders who enthusiastically perform or support the project work, you need to engender trust and respect, perhaps even admiration. It is important to "walk the talk" and establish a consistency in working relationships. For example, if a coach in any sport employs a fiery, demanding style and then abandons it midseason, the team will be confused and confounded, and its performance will likely suffer. Constituents do not expect perfection, but most require consistency from their project leaders. If you adopt this approach, it will have a positive effect on team and stakeholder morale.

....

It is important to "walk the talk" and establish consistency in working relationships.

....

Encouraging Risk Taking and Eliminating the Fear of Failure

As project leader, you should encourage risk taking and try to eliminate the fear of failure. If the team is afraid to make mistakes, its ability to perform at a high level will be impeded. It is important to leverage everyone's knowledge and capability to maximize members' contributions to the project. Although it sounds counterintuitive, mistakes can present important opportunities. Not only can you learn from your mistakes, but you can use them to mold behavior and set the tone of the team environment. During my career as project leader, one of the best practices that I learned was to take advantage of the first mistake I made. I would announce what I did wrong, say, "My bad," and then explain how

I intended to fix the problem. If team members see that you are open and willing to share your missteps, chances are excellent that they will act accordingly and be willing to take prudent risks as the project proceeds.

> Although it sounds counterintuitive, mistakes can present important opportunities. Not only can you learn from your mistakes, but you can use them to mold behavior and set the tone of the team environment.

Establishing a Positive Culture of Dissent

"All titles are left at the door" is one of the first statements I make when meeting with the team for the first time. This is an important ground rule that will help you establish a *positive culture of dissent*. If the project is in the second phase, *storming*, and meetings are overly cordial and agreeable, you have a problem. This is, in all likelihood, a dysfunctional team that is operating in a constricted environment. This does not mean that you encourage conflict, but you will want to promote a variety of perspectives. As project leader, it is important for you to create an environment that encourages the exchange of ideas and opinions, free of the threat of reprisals. This positive culture of dissent helps you keep ideas flowing and assists you in making strategic and tactical decisions. If you are surrounded by "yes" people, devoid of the necessary vetting of ideas, the project will most likely stagnate, and you will lose the real value of your constituents.

Motivation

All project managers require team members to complete activities and accomplish work on time. As an effective project leader, you need to add an additional element—maximum performance. Getting the most from your team requires you to focus on team members as individuals, not just a collective of workers meeting deadlines. If you motivate the individuals, you motivate the team and establish the foundation for a high-performance environment. Conversely, an unmotivated project team will have difficulty succeeding regardless of how the technical aspects of the project are managed.

Some project leads use self-assessment tools to identify traits and possible motivational triggers of the team members. While these have proven to be effective in many instances, I prefer the more traditional approach of spending time with team members and other key stakeholders to find out what makes them tick. If you invest time to speak and listen to team members over coffee on a Tuesday morning (try to avoid Mondays, as some of us need to adjust from the weekend) and acknowledge the contributions of colleagues over a beverage at happy hour or an occasional lunch, you will strengthen the relationship and usually gain insight into who they are. Later in this chapter, I discuss new techniques to apply in today's more challenging virtual and hybrid project worlds. The more you know, the better equipped you will be when the need to motivate arises. MBWA, or management by walking around, was introduced in the 1970s by Bill Hewlett and Dave Packard and became known as the "Hewlett-Packard (HP) style." This technique is still practiced by project leaders, CEOs, and managers at all levels because it works. This is especially true in the typical project environment where the leader is managing without formal authority. If you lack the authority to tell them, you need the ability to motivate them.

Celebrate. As soon as possible, an accomplishment, big or small, should be acknowledged and celebrated as a team. As projects begin, a certain amount of inertia must be overcome. Start by celebrating the small victories, and, as the project progresses, continue to acknowledge good work as appropriate. Many project leaders celebrate with the team as milestones are reached or predetermined goals are accomplished at the end of each project phase. Whichever method you employ, it is your job to keep the momentum going by knowing your team and ensuring high morale.

....

It is your job to keep the momentum going by knowing your team and ensuring high morale.

....

Project Leadership and the Team Environment

As mentioned earlier, the idea of the project manager as leader is a relatively new concept. In the recent past, team member roles, conflict-resolution strategies, and synergies were not considered critical to overall project success. As a project leader today, you need to address all of these areas. This section highlights proven techniques for leading project teams and expands the focus to include distributed virtual teams.

Identifying and Developing Team Member Roles

Although you represent the glue that holds the team together, you can also be thought of as the chef who is responsible for mixing the ingredients of project team member roles, skill sets, and personalities to maximize overall performance. Yes, it's a mixed metaphor, but it illustrates an important concept. As the project progresses, individuals often assume roles that fit naturally into the team environment with little or no resulting conflict. In other cases, it becomes evident that the chemistry is not right, resulting in daily clashes and negative dissent. In today's project world, you need to identify team member strengths, weaknesses, traits, and patterns to establish lasting project rapport. Each team member is present for a purpose, usually functional or subject matter expertise.

In order for the team to gel, you must observe the dynamics of the group. Be proactive and identify danger zones where potential conflicts may occur. Look for opportunities to coordinate team member efforts or even form subteams to leverage their combined talents. Your goal is to promote synergies for maximum team performance. A common definition of *synergy* reads: "The whole is greater than the sum of its parts." As project team leader, this is something for you to strive for, and it is a full-time job.

Determining the Appropriate Approach to Conflict Resolution

All project teams experience conflict at some point, and, as I emphasized earlier, much of it is healthy and positive. It is when conflict becomes destructive to project work and relationships that you need to take action. Personality issues, conflicting priorities, stakeholder disagreement, tight schedules, and technical issues all can be considered root causes of conflict in the project environment. How you deal with the issues that arise will be a determining factor in your effectiveness as project leader. Most of us develop our own styles for dealing with conflict. As mentioned earlier in the chapter, this can lead to a comfort zone that hinders your ability to flex your style to fit the situation. Susan Junda presented five approaches to address conflict in the project environment (*Project Team Leadership: Building Commitment Through Superior Communication*, American Management Association, 2018).

1. *Avoidance.* Often called the *flight syndrome*, avoidance occurs when an individual delays the issue, withdraws from the situation, or avoids the conflict altogether.
2. *Accommodating.* In this instance, an individual focuses on meeting the needs of the other person, to the exclusion of everything else.
3. *Compromising.* This is an attempt to find the *middle ground* in which neither party gets all that it is seeking.

4. *Collaborating.* Here, both parties work together to come to a mutually beneficial solution; this is typically a *win-win* scenario.

5. *Forcing/Competing.* This is the my-way-or-the-highway approach, when one individual forges ahead with his idea.

Your task is to determine which approach is most appropriate given the project conflict scenario. If you have invested yourself in truly understanding your project constituents, this task becomes less difficult. External conflicts require that you make a more thorough assessment of the situation and individual(s) before you make an informed decision. Whichever approach you choose, remember to focus on the facts, not the emotions.

Leading Project Status Meetings

The importance of project status meetings is underrated. Yes, most organizations hold too many meetings that take up too much time, but status meetings are critical to your project's success. If every CEO realized the amount of time and money wasted on inefficient meetings, everybody would be trained to be effective meeting leaders and participants. You as project leader are responsible for making your status meetings efficient, effective, and productive.

....
You as project leader are responsible for making your status meetings efficient, effective, and productive.
....

Here are some best practices for efficiently run project status meetings:

- Prepare in advance; don't expend valuable time accomplishing the work in the meeting.

- Establish meeting ground rules such as:
  - Minimum number of members for a quorum (enough to hold the meeting).
  - Consensus (in case of a deadlock, if five members agree, then the meeting proceeds, with the possibility to revisit the issue).
  - All titles are left at the door (this is worth mentioning again).
  - Confidentiality (everything said stays in the meeting room).
  - One person speaks at a time.
  - Start on time; end on time.
- Appoint a timekeeper to help you keep to your schedule.
- Recruit a scribe to record and distribute meeting minutes.
- Focus on participation to ensure that every voice is heard.
- Do not allow extended sidebar discussions.
- Ensure that all electronic devices are off or on vibrate.

When establishing ground rules, it is important to include all team members to ensure buy-in. If you try to dictate these to the team, nobody will adhere to them. Some project teams alternate the role of scribe. This is a bad idea. If you appoint a single scribe, that individual will develop efficient habits of recording and distributing the minutes in a timely manner. If the job rotates to share the work, each week will produce a different style, and no single team member will develop the efficiencies.

Working with Virtual Teams

"Brussels, we have a problem." I remember saying these words to a team member following my previous decision to suspend weekly videoconferencing. I did not understand the communication challenges that my global team was facing at the time. Needless to say, the decision was reversed. If your team resides in other buildings or is spread across the globe, you should identify your specific challenges and plan to overcome them.

Most virtual teams encounter blockages that are unique or that are much more likely in a geographically dispersed environment. Communication on every level can become an art, a science, a circus, or a torment. When team members are not down the hall or upstairs, clarification can become a project in itself. Things tend to get lost in translation. They fall through the ever-present but often unseen cracks. Add multicultural or multilingual team members, and factions can develop along those lines. Cultural differences, if not identified but left to fester, can prevent the development of real team unity. Differences in work habits, protocol, and style are more common and consequential.

> **Communication on every level can become an art, a science, a circus, or a torment.**

To combat these added challenges, you must go back to basics when it comes to understanding your team members and stakeholders. Insist that the project kickoff meeting be face-to-face. This may prove *very* difficult, especially when extensive travel is involved, but it is crucial to team bonding and future morale. You will find that this is something that must be *sold* to management or the project champion. If this is the case, estimate projected costs and benefits and present them as often as necessary (it once took me six attempts until I got a yes).

If your organization is lacking the latest virtual communication tools, become a squeaky wheel. Sell the need to invest in upgrades by highlighting the costs and negative effects of outdated platforms on previous projects.

As the project progresses, it can also be useful to facilitate as many opportunities for informal interaction among team members as possible. This helps overcome the loss of casual interaction and assists in breaking down barriers. I will explore this approach further in the next section.

The Virtual Project Leader

"Scotty, I need warp speed in three minutes or we're all dead" (*Star Trek: The Wrath of Khan*, Paramount Pictures). Most project managers do not find themselves in such dire circumstances, although it may seem so at times. Most project teams do not have a Scotty they can rely on to save the day every time. No, when things become challenging, we need to adjust and rise to the occasion. Well, things have become challenging. In this new normal of virtual meetings, hybrid communicating, widespread teleworking, and advanced but often unfamiliar technology, effective project leadership requires more focus and dedication than ever. How do you motivate a project team member online with limited interaction? How do you inform and reassure a key stakeholder in this new project environment? What has worked for you in the past may not work today. My advice is to go back to basics and think like a project manager. Assess this new project work environment by asking appropriate questions. What is different in 2022? What are the challenges *and* opportunities that you face? What can you do differently to adjust your approach accordingly? Now you are prepared to create a plan, execute it, and learn.

Plan—Planning is everything. I say that often because when it comes to the management of projects it is so true. When it comes to reinventing your virtual leadership style, a good plan is required. Projects, teams, and organizations vary widely, but I recommend the gap analysis tool to help you identify what must be done to ensure optimal project leader performance. When you construct a gap analysis, identify the current state, the desired state, the gaps between the two, and an action plan to fill in those gaps.

[FIGURE 14-2]
THE GAP ANALYSIS

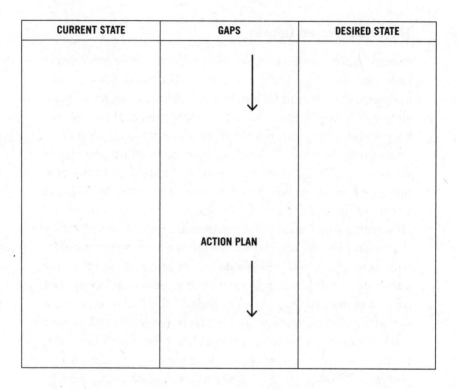

1. The first step of your gap analysis requires you to determine where you are today regarding your project leadership approach.
2. Step two requires you to identify the optimum desired approach to leading your team in today's more virtual, technology-intensive environment.
3. In step three you will identify the gaps between the current and desired state.
4. The final step is where you identify the tasks and subtasks needed to fill in the gaps and reach the desired state. In this case you are filling in the gaps by identifying adjustments you need to make and how you will make them,

to become a more effective virtual project leader. This represents your action plan.

Execute—Now that you have an action plan, it is time to execute it. As with any project, the work required will depend directly on how robust the objective is. That is, the length, width, depth, and breadth of what it is you are trying to accomplish. The action plan resulting from your gap analysis will vary depending on several factors such as industry, size of your organization, access to resources, available technology, budget, and project management training/experience, to name six. Some fortunate project leaders will only be required to make subtle adjustments regarding how they operate. It may be necessary for others to implement a comprehensive plan requiring software purchases and training, enhanced project management training, communication workshops, human resource recruitment, and so on. As you execute your plan, remember the triple constraints triangle and the impact these new approaches may have on your existing project plans (see Chapter 11).

The tendency I have noticed is to skip the planning stage and proceed directly to executing a new approach. Do not do that! This is called winging it, and you will be inviting multiple levels of project pain and sadness. As with all things project related, this plan is an investment in the future—*pay me now or pay me later.* Be proactive! Sell the need for a new approach and put yourself and your project team on a path to success.

Learn—Eventually, leading virtual and hybrid (mixed environment) teams will be so common that project leads, and team members, will become acclimated at "birth," but we are not there yet. As presented in chapter 15, performing a lessons-learned analysis on your project is the most effective way to continuously improve as a project manager. The same concept applies to the project leader planning and executing the transition to a virtual environment. This process alone is a learning experience. Look at your processes and behaviors and identify what has changed. Determine what is working well and what has already been jettisoned (or should be jettisoned) for lack of effectiveness. Try to identify the approaches you can keep and *tweak* to make them more valuable.

Your approach here should be more fluid than with a standard lessons-learned analysis. Whether you have just begun project initiation, you are mid-project, or beginning project closure, you should keep a scorecard of what is working and what needs work in this new environment. Invite comments and suggestions from team members and other stakeholders, as they are learning too. Consider adding a topic to your project status meeting to discuss what you might improve, embrace, or investigate. The need to formalize learning as your projects progress is real, so be sure to apply the scorecard approach as a repeatable project process.

Benchmarking colleagues who lead projects or others in your organization with experience leading virtual teams can be an invaluable source of learning. Great ideas can be found at the watercooler, cafeteria, or through casual conversation. These opportunities are fewer and farther between today, particularly for someone whose team is primarily virtual, so it is necessary to take steps to enhance your benchmarking efforts. Identify those with the most experience in this area and invest some time. Visit online, have coffee, invite them for lunch, or have a beer/soda/ beer (not a typo). Formal benchmarking through an appropriate quality management association such as ASQ can also reap many rewards.

Enhanced Communication

Communication! Communication! Communication! In every project management seminar I lead, this topic surfaces. Everyone agrees that effective communication is crucial for project success, but sadly, few project leaders devote enough time and effort to ensure that it occurs. Today, with virtual and hybrid teams the norm rather than the exception, effective communication becomes more important than before.

To facilitate enhanced communication, I recommend increasing your efforts to fully understand team members and other stakeholders. Some organizations have taken very specific steps toward this end. Hugh Massie (CEO & Founder) and Nikki Evans (Chief Learning Officer) of DNA Behavior International have increased the number of one-on-one calls at their organization. Project leaders at DNA reach out to team members every day or every few days, depending on the requirements of the individual. While project deliverables are discussed, conversations can be extended to gauge how people are feeling and what challenges they may be facing in their new environment.

DNA has also begun to leverage video calls much more than in the past. As we all know, body language and facial expressions matter! Since the implementation of pandemic restrictions, most of my project management seminars have been taught using a virtual platform. When teaching in this environment, I *always* request that seminar participants activate their video camera. Communication capability and training quality are significantly enhanced when I see the participants and they see me. The same concept applies to any project meeting you lead or interaction you have. DNA has also included an occasional show-and-tell when children or pets are introduced. I do the same in my virtual classrooms when these family members wander in. I have found it is an excellent way to enhance our connection. In the absence of kids and pets, try a virtual coffee break or happy hour. The folks at DNA discovered that it helps team members feel connected and creates a shared experience for the team. They have also leveraged chat capability, standardized on a platform, and encouraged real-time sharing. This is highly recommended as it can create the opportunity for "hallway" conversations and combat the loss of casual interaction.

Virtual Platforms

Remote work is not new, but the pandemic has accelerated the shift. Throughout this section of the chapter, we have focused on the adjustments required regarding the way project leaders, teams, and other stakeholders interact. Looking to the future, project leaders must ask, "What technology (tools) will enable these individuals to be most productive and engaged?" "Which tools will work best in my project environment, in my organization?" The answer is not often easy. The most expensive tools may not be the best. The most popular products may not be the best fit for you. The answers to the above questions demand a thorough analysis of your requirements, project management environment, organizational boundaries, and possible solutions. The American Management Association conducted a survey of virtual platforms available today. Here is a partial list for project leaders to consider:

- *Adobe Connect.* Features of Adobe include desktop sharing, messaging, video chat, and digital rooms. Additional capabilities include surveys, whiteboards, and the ability for users to post external content.
- *Cisco Webex Meetings.* This is Cisco's cloud-based web and videoconferencing service that enables virtual teams to collaborate on standards-based video systems and mobile devices. Webex offers various subscription plans with costs tied to specific features.

- *Google Meet.* Previously known as Hangouts Meet, this tool provides enterprise-grade videoconferencing built on Google's secure global infrastructure. Meetings can be joined directly from a calendar event, an email invite, or directly from Gmail.
- *GoToMeeting.* This offers a virtual meeting platform compatible with Windows, Mac, and mobile devices. GoTo allows online screen sharing among participants without the need to download special software. It offers screen sharing via all Chrome web browsers.
- *Microsoft Teams.* This sub-feature of Microsoft Office 365 enables interactive meetings with up to one thousand participants. It also allows room for guests, person-to-person, and team video. Some plans offer screen sharing, an ability to record, and unlimited chat and file sharing.
- *Skype.* Skype is familiar software available on many platforms. It allows video chats and lets you connect one-on-one or with dozens of stakeholders. This tool is popular with small businesses.
- *Virbela.* This is a cloud-based 3D immersive environment providing a virtual reality experience. It offers vast meeting space and can provide a customized workspace with private offices and administrative support. Each user creates an avatar that interacts with other users in real time, regardless of location.
- *Zoom.* This cloud platform for video- and audio conferencing also allows you to conduct webinars and share messages and documents with participants. Zoom also enables mobile screen sharing, HD screen sharing, and the creation of breakout rooms.

But do not just listen to me, or anyone else, for that matter. Do your due diligence! There is a lot to choose from and a lot of overlap. Choosing the best virtual platform for YOU requires some research and a simple matrix. Start by asking a few questions:

What virtual platforms are commonly used at your
   organization?
Do you and your team have access to them?
What are your cost thresholds when choosing a package?
Is training required? If yes, how extensive?
What approvals are required, if any?

Now you can draw your columns and create your decision
matrix:

[FIGURE 14-3]
VIRTUAL DECISION MATRIX

FEATURES	VIRTUAL PLATFORMS				
	A	B	C	D	E
Immersive	X				
Size		X		X	X
Chat		X	X		
Messaging		X	X		
Screen Sharing	X	X	X	X	
Breakout Rooms	X			X	X
Constraints					
Cost	H	M	M	L	L
Training	M	M	H	M	L
Approvals	Y	Y	Y	N	N

X = Satisfies Requirements
H-M-L = High / Med / Low
Y/N = Yes / No
Remember to customize your matrix as appropriate

Many project leaders have found planning, scheduling, and
controlling projects in the virtual or hybrid world can be a challenge. Here are two effective project-specific tools that can help:

Microsoft Project Online. This allows the virtual project leader and team to accomplish what was formerly done in person. Capabilities include team members managing timesheets, reporting task progress, adding new tasks, and adjusting workload with other team members. Virtual leaders and teams can also input information regarding issues and risks, store and work on project documents, and view other projects across the organization.

Project Manager. This is project-specific software that offers planning, time tracking, task and document management, and reporting. Project Manager includes Gantt chart functionality that updates automatically and integrates with many popular platforms.

As we are all aware, the tech landscape changes rapidly, with capability and enhancements in a constant state of flux. Talk to your tech experts, do the research, and invest the effort to create the decision matrix. Good choices here pay off repeatedly in the future.

KEY POINTS TO REMEMBER

- The more agile you become in leading others, the greater the chance for project success.
- It is important to "walk the talk" and establish consistency in your working relationships. Encouraging risk taking, eliminating fear of failure, and establishing a positive culture of dissent will make you a more effective project leader.
- It is your job to keep the momentum going by knowing your team and ensuring high morale.
- Virtual project leaders require enhanced communication practices and a familiarity with appropriate virtual platforms.
- As a project leader, you need to be able to identify and develop team member roles, determine the appropriate approach to

conflict resolution, lead project status meetings, and work with virtual teams.

EXERCISE

Analyze the project environment in your organization.

► Make a list of ten important project leadership characteristics that help ensure success.
► From that list, identify the three most important characteristics.
► Then, contrast the list with your own abilities.

Which characteristics are your strongest?

Which areas may need improvement?

CHAPTER 15

CLOSING THE PROJECT

Most project managers do not close their projects well. And once again, while the processes and tools are not difficult to understand, the actual goal is not always easy to accomplish. Project closure takes discipline. Think about an experience you may have had. What happens when you approach the finish line of a race? Many of us experience a letdown, slowing as we cross the line. What happens when you or your partner approach the end of a home improvement project? There is a small corner of my den ceiling that, after three and a half years, still remains unpainted. The rest of the room looks great!

When you near the end of a project and enter the closure phase, keep in mind that discipline is the key. You may have been working the project for six months, a year, or even five years, and as a result may be bored with it. Perhaps you are working on other projects as well, one of which has an approaching deadline while another has its critical path in deep trouble (see chapter 8). Perhaps you have functional work that your manager is calling and emailing you about, asking for updates. There could be any number of reasons why you want to move on, but my years in project management have taught me to slow down and manage my project carefully and deliberately, right through to the finish line.

Two Types of Project Closure

Project closure activities are generally broken into two main categories, contractual and administrative. There can be overlap between the two categories, but contractual closure typically involves formal documents, while administrative closure is multifaceted.

Contractual closure brings to completion just what you might expect: contracts, purchase orders, third-party agreements, and the like. Most external activities will fit in this category.

Administrative closure brings to completion all internal aspects of the project. This includes:

- *Turning Over the Deliverable.* Although it may seem like common sense, more than once I have seen a project team do an outstanding job and enter celebration mode, only to realize that the project *product* had not yet been delivered to the customer. Technically, at that point in time, the project was late. In one case, the project's late status triggered monetary penalties. When the deliverable is not turned over, it is usually because nobody *owned* the task. *Remember, your project is not completed until the customer signs off on the deliverable.*

- *Creating Team Member Performance Documentation.* Some project team members will exceed expectations and perform exceptionally well. Others may "ride the team" with very little impact on project work. Be sure to reward the top performers. This can be done by awarding a bonus or a gift certificate or by sending a commendation letter regarding the individual to senior management. You may want to work with your human resources department to design an appropriate show of appreciation. This can be an investment in the future because you may work with these team members again, and you want them to be motivated when that day comes.

- *Gathering and Archiving Project Records in a Project Information and Document Repository.* It is, of course, important to close out your current project, but gathering and archiving project records can also be useful for future, similar projects. Do not let your experiences (good and bad) be lost forever to the uncertainty of your memory. Typical records archived should include your:
  - Project plan
  - Correspondence
  - Change control log
  - Risk register
  - Action/issue logs
  - Quality documentation
  - Communication plan
  - Project procurement report
- *Releasing the Project Team.* You want to create a smooth transition for team members and their functional managers after your project. Remember, you may be sharing these same resources again. Once the project work is complete, you want to be sure that your human resources (your team members) are charged back to their functional department, not to your project. Timely and accurate release of the project team is important here.
- *Summarizing Post-completion Variance Data.* This includes the project's:
  - Scope
  - Schedule
  - Budget

  This will help you understand your project performance *and* begin documenting your experience for future projects.

Did you experience scope creep? Did you finish ahead of schedule or over budget?

- *Closing All Reports, Including Financials.* You do not want to leave any loose ends. I once received a phone call from a Northrop Grumman employee about a year after I had left the company. He was asking for a signature on a financial report for a project that had ended just after I had left. It was an awkward phone call, but in that instance I was able to point him to my successor. You may not be as lucky.
- *Forwarding Regulatory Reports to the Appropriate Agencies.* Some industries and projects are highly regulated. If your project fits this category, make sure you have identified clear team member ownership for these tasks to be accomplished.
- *Thanking Your Stakeholders.* This is a good habit to fall into, as many current stakeholders may become future stakeholders as well. It is amazing what a simple phone call or email can do to solidify future relationships.
- *Identifying and Charting Lessons Learned.* Be sure to analyze what went right and what could have been done better regarding your completed project.

> There are generally two kinds of project closure activities: *contractual closure*, which involves formal documents, and *administrative closure*, which involves bringing to completion all external aspects of the project.

Creating a Project Information and Documentation Repository

Project managers should create a central repository for all project information and documents. In the past, we used accordion files to chart a project's path as it matured and the volume of information and documents increased. I will assume that you now have an electronic file on your desktop for this purpose.

> **Project managers should create a central storehouse for all project information and documents.**

Today, organizations use information systems of varying sophistication and capability to store project information and documentation. In 2022, you may typically have access to a shared drive, a file directory, a file cabinet, and/or a specific software database, or anything in *the cloud*.

The important point here is to use the information technology that your organization provides to create a central repository. You can set this up on your PC, laptop, tablet, or even your smartphone (depending on propriety of the data). Create your repository, feed it regularly, and remember to have *redundant* backup, both technological and team based. Your system can crash, and your team members may leave. You do not want to lose your project history.

Creating a Lessons-Learned Analysis

The easiest way to continuously improve as a project manager is to conduct a lessons-learned analysis. Your organization may call it a postmortem; I used to call it a post-project audit or lessons-learned analysis. Whatever term you use to describe it, this analysis must be accomplished during project closure so that you can build on your experiences and grow as a project manager. Figure 15-1 offers an example of such an analysis.

[FIGURE 15-1]

LESSONS-LEARNED ANALYSIS

ID	Type	Item	Description	Comments
1	Improve	Communications	More frequent status updates are required; correspondence must be more efficient.	Create common plan.
2	Improve	PERT duration estimates (See chapter 7)	Schedule estimates were overly optimistic.	Adjust PERT duration estimates for better accuracy.
3	Embrace	Risk management	Most risks were captured by the risk management plan; contingency plans were effective and implemented in a timely manner.	N/A
4	Embrace	WBS construction	Project scope was well defined—limited scope creep.	N/A

As you can see, the lessons-learned chart is simple by design, but it is not always easy to complete. While it is always satisfying to remember what went right during the project, it can be painful to remember the mistakes. It takes a certain amount of introspection on the part of the project manager and team to do this well. This is an example of the project manager as leader; you must motivate your team to work hard during this analysis by emphasizing continuous improvement and personal growth for all. You and your team must work together to construct a thorough chart and improve after each project.

I recommend that you create your lessons-learned chart during your penultimate meeting. This will ensure that you and your team will not lose momentum and will not be forced to refocus on your previous project after you have moved on to other work. Many project managers wait until the project is completed and the dust settles, but I find this ineffective.

A lessons-learned analysis helps emphasize
continuous improvement and personal growth for
both the project manager and team.

I also encourage my team to keep a contemporary list of improve/
embrace items as the project matures through its life cycle. This
affords us a head start on creating the chart and becomes the back-
bone of the agenda for the lessons-learned meeting. Do not wait
until the last meeting. *Save the last meeting for a celebration!* Even if
the project was not wildly successful—or even if it was worse than
that—celebrate the hard work that the team accomplished.

Here are three final recommendations:

1. You may want to segregate your *improve/embrace* items in
   separate groups, as shown in figure 15-1. This is typically
   a style choice and depends on your personal preference.
2. Highlight *improve* items in red, *embrace* items in green.
   This is not only a quick reference aide, but it fits in well
   with the *stoplight* (red/yellow/green) tracking approach
   that is common in today's project environment.
3. Create a comprehensive project management lessons-
   learned database on your organization's intranet. If you
   are in a position of power, deem it necessary. If your posi-
   tional power is low, perhaps you can be the prime mover
   for this effort. Encourage all project managers to con-
   tribute improve and embrace items. This is typically done
   anonymously, as most of us tend to be reluctant to broad-
   cast our mistakes honestly across the organization. That's
   okay; I have enjoyed much success implementing this
   idea working with organizations in my consulting practice. I simply stress the fact that everybody learns from
   each other, and a rising tide lifts all boats.

Reviewing Your Project Closure Checklist

When you finally get to the end of your project, it may have been weeks, months, or years since work on it began. You want to celebrate with your team, but you know you cannot yet. You have not reviewed your project closure checklist. I never rest until the checklist is reviewed and all actions are confirmed complete. This is the second closure activity that I recommend accomplishing during the penultimate meeting (after your lessons-learned analysis). If the lessons-learned analysis consumes the entire next-to-last meeting, then you should set up a separate meeting for creating your project review checklist. It is that important.

A project should not be considered finished until a project closure checklist has been completed.

Many years ago, I learned a best practice that I apply when creating my project closure checklists.

First, as shown in figure 15-2, you create a list of actions that will apply to closing out all projects that you manage. This will be the *core* of your checklist and can vary in size depending on your typical project work.

Next, continue to add to this list of actions as the project matures and grows throughout the life cycle.

For example:

- *End of Phase I.* Add two actions that must be accomplished and confirmed during project closure.
- *End of Phase II.* Add one action.
- *End of Phase III.* Add three actions.

By the end of the project, during project closure, you will have created an all-inclusive, comprehensive checklist of actions. You

[FIGURE 15-2]
PROJECT CLOSURE CHECKLIST

Item	Owner	Action	Status
1	Steven	Internal documentation complete/archived	X
2	Laurie	All change requests have been closed/archived	?
3	Rocco	All financials closed out	X
4	Rocco	All project contracts are closed	X
5	Molly	All technical documentation is complete	X
6	Project Manager	Client/customer signs off on project deliverables	X
7	Steven	Project celebration has been scheduled	X

X = Completed

? = Unknown

and your team will then review your performance during the project and confirm that all actions are complete. By doing this, you and your team will improve by having answered the question "How did we do?" It has been my experience that, almost invariably, one or two actions will be questionable. Occasionally, while reviewing the questionable actions, the project team will discover that an item was not completed. Perhaps nobody owned the task, or two team members did, assuming the other did the work. Whatever the reality, this is a powerful redundancy check (a recurring theme during project closure) for you and the team to be sure that all necessary actions have been accomplished.

Now you can wrap the project up and move on. Do not admire your work too long, however, because you probably have two other projects working and one in the queue.

Dealing with Premature Project Closure

Projects are terminated or canceled early all the time. The reasons necessitating early closure can be many and varied. The most common reasons I have either experienced or observed usually involve one or some of the following:

- The project has been deprioritized because of shifting priorities in the organization.
- The project has run out of money, and the well is dry.
- A shift in market forces has rendered the project deliverable obsolete.
- Organizational politics have led to project cancellation.
- It has become clear that the project deliverable will not work or will fall short of expectations.
- It has become clear that the technology does not work.
- Your boss or project sponsor has changed his mind.
- Your project life is jinxed. (This reason is not real, but this has crossed all our minds from time to time.)

Whatever the reason, the project must still be closed out as any full-term project is. This calls for the creation of an early termination/cancellation, as shown in figure 15-3. You must complete all of the tasks necessary during the closure, just as you would with any other project. The only difference is the premature closure.

A project must be closed out whether it has been completed or terminated or canceled.

This chart emphasizes the fact that the project manager and team must formally close the project regardless of when early termination occurs. This should include all the steps presented in this chapter. As always, make sure that you and your team take a formal approach when implementing the closure process.

[FIGURE 15-3]
EARLY TERMINATION/CANCELLATION CHART

KEY POINTS TO REMEMBER

▶ Be disciplined! Most project managers skim over the closure process too quickly. Adhere to the closure processes.

▶ Perform all contractual and administrative closure activities.

▶ Create a central information and documentation repository.

▶ Perform a lessons-learned analysis. Build on your successes, and avoid making the same mistakes again.

▶ Create and review your project closure checklist.

▶ Remember, your project is not complete until the customer signs off.

▶ Celebrate!!!

CHAPTER 16

PROJECT RECOVERY

I f your title is project manager (PM) or you occasionally manage projects as an accidental project manager, you have probably uttered the words, "I'm in trouble." I certainly have said them more than I care to remember. As a young man managing projects, I was a PM in name only. I had not been trained and it is more accurate to say that my projects were managing me. An issue would arise, and I would react. A change would impact the project and I would overreact. Managing projects in this manner, I was more accurately a firefighter attempting to stomp out fires as they appeared. This is a *bad* idea and often put me in the position of managing a troubled project, or project failure.

Once trained, I discovered that many good projects going bad can be saved if the correct steps are taken with a structured approach to recovery. I also learned that remaining calm and exhibiting control can be crucial to successful recovery. If you lose control, you relinquish control.

The symptoms will be clear—your schedule is slipping, budget thresholds have been exceeded, the scope of the project has crept unmercifully, or perhaps resources have been stretched beyond recognition. Since these project constraints are interrelated (see chapter 11), you may experience all of the above occurring simultaneously. Regardless of your specific project crisis, remember, do *not* treat the symptoms. This will likely result in a short-term correction but will not make the project healthy. If a patient has a fever and the doctor prescribes an aspirin, the fever will be reduced (a temporary correction) but the patient may die because the underlying cause was not identified and treated. In our project example, more time or money may feel good, but the project may fail because you never understood what was causing the schedule to slip or your budget to explode. Therefore, you begin the project recovery process with *questions* to determine the causes of your project grief. When you gain a better understanding of the situation, then, and only then, should you move forward identifying possible solutions. Now you can make an informed decision regarding how to proceed and create a formal recovery plan. Once your plan is complete, you must solicit buy-in from appropriate stakeholders (boss, sponsor, steering committee) then implement your plan. Remember, project recovery is a process, which means structure is required and progress can be monitored.

The FADE Process

When I lead project management recovery seminars or wear my consultant's hat helping an organization correct course regarding a troubled project, I typically rely on the FADE process to guide the way. I was introduced to FADE while leading a team at Grumman Aerospace tasked with implementing a new supplier performance rating system. The FADE process is a popular quality improvement model and is often used for focused process improvement, in addition to project recovery. As with most project management processes, FADE is effective for its relative simplicity and agility as it can be applied to any project, at any level, and in any industry.

Here is the FADE process adjusted for project recovery:

[FIGURE 16-1]
THE FADE PROCESS

FOCUS	ANALYZE	DEVELOP	EXECUTE

Identify Project	Collect Data	Generate Solutions	Acquire Buy-In
Problems/Variances	Identify Patterns	Select a Solution	Execute Plan
	Identify Root Causes	Develop a Recovery Plan	Monitor Recovery

Focus. Questions are the tools as you begin the FADE process. As mentioned, you cannot begin the recovery effort until you understand what the problems are. To do this, start with your project performance baselines. There are three major performance baselines—scope, schedule, and budget—which are also the three sides of the triple constraints triangle (see chapter 11). Remember, the *baseline* is the most recently approved version of your project plan. Refer to your baseline plan to answer the following questions:

- Where *should* the project be per my baseline, as of today?
- Where is the project today?
- What are the current performance variances per my baselines?

In short, variances between the baseline plan and actual status of the project are identified. You are determining if you are ahead, behind, or very close to where you expect to be. The American Management Association presents three simple but effective calculations toward this end in the seminar Improving Your Project Management Skills; the Basics for Success:

SCHEDULE VARIANCE (SV)

SV = baseline (planned) completion date–actual completion date

COST VARIANCE (CV) PERSONNEL / EXPENSES

Personnel CV = baseline (planned) personnel costs–actual personnel costs

Expense CV = baseline (planned) expense costs–actual expense costs

I add project scope variance during this portion of FADE as many troubled projects can trace their troubles to *scope creep* (see chapter 3). I use estimated percentage of variance from planned scope to determine scope variance:

SCOPE VARIANCE (SCV)

ScV = baseline (planned) scope of work–current actual scope of work

Extreme schedule slippage will be self-evident and easy to identify. More robust projects might require some research and reaching out to subject matter experts (SMEs) and/or project stakeholders. As outlined above, cost variance focuses on the two primary cost factors for most projects: personnel and expenses. Other cost factors may be involved so your approach should be flexible. A thorough analysis and comparison of planned vs. actual scope of work will allow you to assign a percentage variance, more or less scope, from the plan. Calculating these project performance variances will help identify where the problems are and where your focus should be as you proceed to the analyze phase of FADE.

Analyze. Now that you have a better understanding of your project challenges, it is time to identify patterns and analyze causes and related factors. Effective data gathering during this portion of FADE will assist you in confirming your focus and create the foundation for developing possible solutions. It is now time to dig deeper into the performance variances developed during Focus. Remember, the project is doing poorly so there will be a tendency to skip this step and proceed straight to developing solutions. *Don't do it!* At this point, discipline, structure, and a calm approach can be indispensable in correcting what is negatively affecting your project.

There is a reason most experienced project managers understand that planning is everything when it comes to managing successful projects. Your project is floundering but now that you seek data for recovery, your original project plan can be your best friend. As you research data, look to your project plan for answers. Start at the beginning, always a good idea, with a review of the project charter. This will include initial scope definition as well as many other foundational project elements (see chapter 1). Proceed through your project plan and research data that may relate to previously identified performance variances. Your research could involve reviewing PERT estimates (see chapter 7), critical and noncritical path tasks, resource allocation and resource loading matrices, supplier performance, and other areas of the plan. Review the stakeholder grid to determine who might be negatively affecting the project and/or whose influence you might leverage during project recovery. I also recommend reviewing communication throughout the project and the effectiveness of your change control process. As always, a good project plan will contain a comprehensive risk management plan (see chapter 6). Refer to this and you may be rewarded with multiple contingencies that you have already established to correct performance variances. These are more examples of time and effort invested (not spent) being paramount to project success, even if the project falters.

In many cases, root causes of problems affecting your project will need to be identified. I reserve root cause analysis for problems that are expected to recur if nothing is done to correct them. If allowed to recur, these problems will become an anchor around the recovery process and you will find yourself treating symptoms, not underlying causes. The most effective and often used root cause analysis tool is the fishbone diagram:

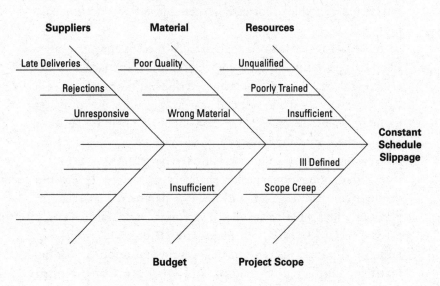

[FIGURE 16-2]

THE FISHBONE DIAGRAM

To construct a fishbone diagram, place the problem to be diagnosed at the head of the fish, then draw a straight line extending back with ribs branching off above and below. At the end of each rib, identify major cause categories then decompose the major causes to identify possible root causes. Display these as smaller bones extending from each rib. This is typically created through brainstorming with team members and SMEs. If it is unlikely that the problem will recur, skip the fishbone analysis and proceed to the next step of FADE. You can then begin developing possible solutions. For this type of problem, root causes can be identified during a lessons-learned review.

Develop. Confident of your focus and armed with insight from your analysis, you are ready to develop possible solutions to accomplish full recovery of your project. If the solution is obvious, great. You can proceed to the Execute phase with confidence. However, in most cases multiple solutions will have been identified and decisions must be made. Do *not* make these decisions in a vacuum. At this point of the FADE process, I recommend calling a formal recovery meeting (virtual or otherwise) including team members, SMEs, and appropriate stakeholders. I cannot emphasize more strongly the importance of different perspectives and the process of weighing the costs/benefits of implementing each solution. It is in situations like these that a positive culture of dissent (see chapter 14) is most important. Remember, the environment will typically still be frantic with fingers pointing and anxiety levels rising. Continue to rely on process and a professional, steady approach as you proceed. Again—if you lose control, you relinquish control.

The next step in this phase is to develop a recovery plan. The nature of project recovery plans can vary significantly, with some necessitating simple adjustments to one or more aspects of the original project plan. Recovery on the other end of the spectrum will require a separate plan for rehabilitating the project, with many scenarios requiring a combined approach. Choosing the correct approach is important and demands focus as circumstances will change and flexibility will be required.

The good news is that project managers are planners, by nature or necessity. The best method for developing the recovery plan is by using the planning tools that you have honed and become familiar with managing previous projects. Once an agreed-upon solution is chosen, begin the recovery plan by creating a work breakdown structure or WBS (see chapter 7). This is a familiar tool that all readers should recognize and, done correctly, will identify all the work that needs to be accomplished to achieve project recovery per the chosen solution. As with any project plan, the recovery plan should include estimated task durations and schedule adjustments including impact on the critical path, projected resource requirements, budget impact projections, and a good risk analysis. The risk analysis should include the question

"What is the risk of doing nothing?" The implementation of any solution should not be more painful than the problem. Therefore, as the planned solution will be an investment of time, effort, people, and/or money, it must not impact the project more negatively than the current challenges it faces.

Execute. The three major steps of execution involve acquiring buy-in, implementing the plan, and monitoring the recovery. Acquiring buy-in is not unlike presenting a business case for a project (reasons why a project should be approved) or presenting project progress to your boss, steering committee, or senior management. It is here that you rely on the hard work that has already been invested throughout the FADE process and use it to *persuade* the decision-makers of the soundness of the recovery plan. Come prepared with your best possible presentation and presenter (possibly a team member) and let the data do the talking. Causes of the current state of the troubled project are typically requested so a review is appropriate and may include a fishbone diagram. However, most of the focus should be devoted to recovery and your plan to achieve it, including time, resources, and other notable requirements. Typically, a fair amount of negotiation will occur, so come prepared!

Once the green light is given, execution of the recovery plan can begin. Your existing team or project support network will often be sufficient to implement the plan successfully. In some recovery situations, it may be necessary to recruit SMEs external to the project on a part-time or more dedicated basis. If you are facing a more robust recovery scenario, a satellite or *tiger* team may be required to achieve maximum speed, quality, and efficiency. This team approach is usually reserved for more extreme scenarios when the troubled project is resulting in a severe negative impact on the organization. The tiger team should be compact (five members or fewer) and managed as any other project team. This team should also have a single point of contact with the primary project team to maximize effective communication.

As the recovery plan is executed, progress must be monitored as with any other project. I have yet to see a project plan of any significant size survive intact, so execution of your plan involves the familiar cycle of performing the work and revisiting the plan for probable revisions. At this point, I am reminded of the boxer/philosopher Mike Tyson who is alleged to have said, "Every boxer starts off with a plan until he gets punched in the face." While I do not want you to think of your project as an opponent, it is true we sometimes get hit in the face, especially during project recovery. As you monitor the execution of your recovery plan, keep your finger on the pulse of the plan and an eye on overall project performance. Go back to basics by tracking scope, schedule, budget, resources, and their associated performance baselines. As you try to get your project back on track, make sure you are staying on track.

Remember, most project recovery efforts occur *on the fly*, to borrow an ice hockey phrase. In ice hockey, a team may need to change players while the action continues instead of waiting for a stoppage of play. As you shuffle human resources on the fly, your project leadership skills (see chapter 14) will be tested, and it is important to monitor individual and team morale. In some cases, you will be forced to take extreme action and halt the project while corrections are made. This is the second most difficult decision you may be forced to make during project recovery. Reasons for taking this action can be many and varied but should be undertaken when the data collected and reality of the situation indicate that it is unfeasible to proceed with the project while corrections are made. Now for the most difficult decision you may be forced to make . . .

Project Termination

When I conduct informal polls while leading project management seminars, I will ask participants about their most difficult decisions, and this decision usually wins. Yes, a project is work but it can also become your *baby*, especially if months of time and effort have been devoted to its successful completion. You can become attached. Many years ago, as a young project manager, I recommended continuing more than one troubled project that I knew I should terminate. This always had a negative effect on me, my project team, and the organization. The point, is it is not always an easy thing to do. Regardless of the obvious logic supporting termination, there can always be that nagging sense of failure when your project is canceled. Learn from my early mistakes, do not fall into this trap, and make the tough decision when appropriate.

Causes for termination may include starvation by budget restrictions, deprioritization by senior management, technical advances that make the project deliverable obsolete, cost escalations affecting viability of the deliverable, organizational downsizing, and the dreaded mismanagement of the project. When it becomes clear that the decision to terminate must be made— *punt.* I am probably breaking rules by mixing multiple metaphors (sports metaphors!) in this chapter, but punting is so appropriate here that I must use it to illustrate the positive effect of terminating a troubled project that should not be rehabilitated. And, after all, it is *my* book. In American football if a team has failed to acquire a certain amount of territory after three plays (10 yards or 9.144 meters), they can terminate their control of the football and punt it back to the other team, rather than trying one last play. Yes, they stop trying to score for their team, but it is temporary. They will limit the damage and have an opportunity to score again later in the game. Think of project termination as an opportunity to punt. Rather than spending and perhaps wasting time, people, money, and material on a project that has limited probability of adding value to the organization, recommend canceling the project. You and your team will live to initiate and manage other projects and all your efforts can be redirected toward that end. Make this decision as soon as it becomes apparent as the most appropriate course of action any time during the FADE process, prior to acquiring buy-in. I have found that it is better to recommend than be told.

KEY POINTS TO REMEMBER

- Do not treat symptoms of a troubled project.
- Invest time and effort to identify why the project is failing.
- Rely on the FADE process to structure your recovery.
- FADE will help you focus on the problem, analyze pertinent data, develop possible solutions, and execute a recovery plan.
- Monitor corrective actions during execution to ensure effective implementation of the plan.
- Make the often-difficult decision to recommend termination of a project that has little or no chance for success.

CHAPTER 17

HOW TO MAKE PROJECT MANAGEMENT WORK IN YOUR COMPANY

I t is one thing to know how to manage projects. It is another to get people to actually *do* the work of the project. Flying by the seat of your pants seems a lot easier than doing all the planning, scheduling, and monitoring that have been presented in this book. Even when people invest three or four days in project management seminars, you find that they soon forget what they have been taught and go back to their old ways.

I have struggled with this problem for more than twenty years and finally have some answers. Here are suggestions on how to make the principles of project management work in your company:

- Dr. W. Edwards Deming learned more than fifty years ago that if you don't get top management involved in a program, the program will be short-lived. This doesn't mean just having them pay lip service to it. As Tom Peters suggests in his book *Thriving on Chaos* (Harper Perennial, 1988), if an executive wants something to happen in the company, she has to change her calendar; she must spend time talking about project management, sit in on project planning or review meetings, start asking to see people's project notebooks, and ask questions about how projects are doing. In other words, she must show an interest in the subject.

- Companies must build into performance appraisals items that evaluate a project manager's use of the best management tools. They should reward people for practicing the best methods and, if necessary, sanction them when they do not. But be careful. Be sure upper management is not keeping managers from practicing good methodology.

- It helps to have the entire team trained in the basics. After all, when you tell members of your team that you want them to do a WBS for their part of the project and they've never even heard the term before, they can't very well deliver. I have found that project managers generally need a minimum of three or four days' training in project management, and team members need about two days' training.

- I have found that senior management should have a brief overview of the principles so that it knows what is realistic to expect. One of the most common causes of project failures is unrealistic expectations on the part of senior managers. However, I have found that most senior managers are so busy that you can get them together for only about three hours—if you can even do that. We have finally videotaped a briefing and cut it down to one hour and fifteen minutes, just enough time for busy executives to learn what they need to know to support and drive the effort. Today, senior managers should take advantage of the many online training options available to them.

- After the training is complete, pick a project that already has a pretty high probability of success—don't pick your hardest job; the probability of failure is too high—and have your trainer/consultant walk the team through the steps. This is the hand-holding phase, and I have found it to be essential (as have a number of major companies with which I have worked). It really helps to have someone assist the team in practicing what it has learned. All new procedures feel awkward when you first try them, and an outside expert makes things go smoother. In addition, an outsider can be more objective than members of the team.

- Plan small wins for people. Forget the Pareto principle. It's wrong in this particular instance, even from an economic point of view. According to Pareto, you should begin with your most important problems and solve them, then move on to the simpler ones. Sounds like good economic sense, but it isn't. It ignores the fact that the biggest problem is also likely to be the hardest to tackle, so people are more likely to fail, become demoralized, and give up. No sports team ranked tenth would want to play the top-ranked team for its first game. It would prefer to play the ninth-ranked team maybe, or even the eleventh. Don't set the team up to be slaughtered!

- Practice a lot of MBWA (management by walking around) as the project progresses, but do it to be helpful, not in the blame-and-punishment mode. Give people kudos for letting you know about problems early, not after they have turned into disasters. Don't be too quick to help people, though. Give them time to solve the problems themselves. Just ask them to keep you informed, and tell them to let you know if they need help. Be a resource, not the police.

- Do process reviews to learn and to try to improve whenever possible.

- If you find you have a problem child on your team, deal with that person as soon as possible. If you don't know how to handle the problem, talk to someone who has the experience and who can help you. Don't ignore the problem, as it can wreck your entire team.

- Be very *proactive*, not reactive. Take the lead. Break roadblocks for your team members. Go to bat for them.

- Have team members make presentations to senior management on their parts of the job. Give them credit for their contributions. Build ownership.

- If you are running a project where people are assigned temporarily but still report to their own bosses (the matrix organization), keep their managers informed about what they are doing. Try to build good relations with those managers. You may need their support to get the job done.

- For those tasks on the critical path of the project, you may find that you have to strategically locate the people doing those activities so that you don't have them constantly pulled off to do other jobs. Major corporations are using this method more and more today on highly important projects.

- It may be useful to consider setting up a *project support person* or office to do all scheduling for your project managers. Rather than have everyone try to master the software, it may be better to train one or two people to competence level, with users trained only enough to know the capability of the software. Under this scenario, project managers give raw data to the support group, which enters them into the computer and then gives back the schedule; the schedule is then massaged until it works. Subsequently, the support group does all updates, what-if analyses, and so on for the project manager.

- Along this line, have a person assigned as *project administrator*. This person either does the project support or delegates it. He also sits in on project review meetings, holds the team's hands to walk members through planning and audits, and so forth. Naturally, you need to be running quite a few projects (at least ten to twenty) to justify this position. Such a person can be helpful when the people who are managing projects have little experience with managing or perhaps have poor skills for dealing with people, or both.

- Benchmark other companies to find out what they do with project management. Note that, when you find companies that don't practice good methodology, this does not give you grounds for abandoning good practices yourself. I know of one major corporation that does not track actual work put into a project, yet the company is extremely successful. Very likely, the fact that it doesn't track work is going to lead to problems eventually. The company does a lot of other things really well, however, and I would not hesitate to benchmark those things.

- Have individuals take responsibility for being *champions* of various parts of the project management process. Perhaps you can make one person the earned value champion, who goes around the company trying to get everyone on board so that all team members use the same method. Another could take responsibility for dealing with WBS notation, and so on.

- Join the Project Management Institute, attend its chapter meetings, and learn more about project management from other professionals.

- Try to read current management books, and glean everything you can from them that will help you do your job better. Managing projects is a demanding job, and you need all the help you can get.

- Consider changing the structure of the organization to one that is project-based. Tell all functional managers that they exist to serve the needs of projects. Many of them will scream. Some may even quit. But, in today's world, where most of what gets done in organizations is in project format, this makes good sense.

- Set up a project management function, with dedicated project managers. You don't have everyone doing accounting. Not everyone is good at it. This is also true of project management. By making it a function, like all the others, you provide a way for dedicated individuals to hone their skills and get really good at their jobs. An excellent resource for this is *Creating an Environment for Successful Projects* (Berrett-Koehler, 2019), by Robert Graham and Randall L. Englund.

- Look at managing projects as a *challenge* or even as a game. If it doesn't strike you that way, it probably won't be very exciting. Experiment with new approaches. Find out what works, and keep it. Throw out what does not.

Finally—good luck!

ACKNOWLEDGMENTS

A special thanks to Nicolle Heagney for her technical assistance in creating many of the figures and charts presented in the book. Her expertise and diligence made my life a lot easier, again.

Thanks to Kyle Heagney for graduating on time and within budget, again (law school).

ANSWERS TO EXERCISES

Chapter 1

1. c
2. d
3. a
4. b

Chapter 3

You should decide on project strategy before you begin implementation planning. At that point, you should develop tactics to execute strategy and plan logistics so that people will have what they need to execute the tactics.

Chapter 5

Check your work for:
Prioritization factors: probability and impact.

Remember:
Some risks cannot be prevented, but they can be mitigated.
Your contingencies should represent specific actions if the risk occurs.
Your trigger points should relate directly to a contingency.

Chapter 7

WBS for camping trip:

[FIGURE A-1]

WBS FOR THE CAMPING TRIP

Chapter 8

Solution to the WBS exercise:

[FIGURE A-2]

ARROW DIAGRAM FOR HOUSE CLEANING

Chapter 9

Solution to the scheduling exercise:

[FIGURE A-3]

SOLUTION FOR SCHEDULING EXERCISE

Chapter 11

Refer to the chapter to check your responses regarding a change to your project.

Chapter 12

1. It is behind schedule by $160 worth of work.
2. It is overspent by $240.
3. It will be overspent by $416.

Chapter 14

You can use this exercise as you would a post-project "lessons-learned analysis." Reinforce your strongest project leadership characteristics—work to improve characteristics where you are deficient.

INDEX

ABOUT THE AUTHORS

Joseph Heagney has been president of QMA International, LLC, since 2001, providing a wide range of management learning solutions worldwide. He specializes in delivering seminars to Fortune 500 companies and speaking at selected conferences and conventions. His clients have included PepsiCo, Federal Express, Verizon, Merck, Harvard Business School, the US Armed Forces, and SAP Americas.

Mr. Heagney joined the American Management Association International (AMA) in 1996 as a program manager overseeing manufacturing, quality, and purchasing public seminar product lines. Following a transition to the project management product line, he was named group program manager for the Center for Management Development in New York City and managed program managers in the areas of project management, training and development, communication, purchasing, and general management. Promoted to global practice leader, project management best practices, he led an international team responsible for identifying and then incorporating best practices into AMA learning solutions content worldwide.

He is also an adjunct instructor at the City University of New York Graduate Center, teaching multiple project management MBA courses. Mr. Heagney was formerly an adjunct instructor with Dowling College, New York, teaching in their Executive MBA Program. Courses taught include Project Management, Production and Operations Management, Operations Research, Leadership, General Management, Human Management Systems, Total Quality Management, Statistical Quality/Statistical Process Control, and Executive Development.

He began his career with Grumman Aerospace (Northrop Grumman), where he advanced through the Material Management and Corporate Procurement divisions. He completed his career at Northrop Grumman leading a project team to create and implement a corporate-wide supplier performance rating system.

Mr. Heagney holds a bachelor of science degree in education from C.W. Post College and a master of science degree in industrial management from SUNY Stony Brook. His professional affiliations have included the Project Management Institute, the International Project Management Association, and the American Society for Quality.

Fundamentals of Project Management would not be the best-selling title it is without James P. Lewis, PhD, the author of the first three editions. Dr. Lewis is president of the Lewis Institute, Inc., a training and consulting company specializing in project management, which he founded in 1981. An experienced project manager, he has conducted seminars worldwide and has trained more than forty thousand individuals since 1981.

Jim Lewis is the author of ten books, including *Project Planning, Scheduling and Control, Mastering Project Management, The Project Manager's Desk Reference, Working Together: The 12 Principles Employed by Boeing Commercial Aircraft to Manage Projects, Teams, and the Organization*, published by McGraw-Hill, and *How to Build and Manage a Winning Project Team and Team-Based Project Management*, published by AMACOM Books. He is also coauthor, with Bob Wysocki, of *The World-Class Project Manager*, published by Perseus.